GALA MORA & CAROLINA AMELL

# IBIZA INTERIORS

Lannoo

# CONTENTS

## 01
### COSMOPOLITAN

| | |
|---|---|
| 10 | OUT OF THE BLUE |
| 20 | STARTING FROM SCRATCH |
| 34 | ADAPT AND THRIVE |
| 48 | COOL, CALM AND COLLECTED |

## 02
### ECLECTIC

| | |
|---|---|
| 58 | A PLACE OF ONE'S OWN |
| 72 | A CAREFULLY CRAFTED CASA |
| 82 | BETWEEN TWO SEAS |

## 03
### MEDITERRANEAN

| | |
|---|---|
| 94 | HOME AT LAST |
| 106 | A SENSE OF CRAFT |
| 118 | THE GREAT OUTDOORS |
| 130 | THE ESSENCE OF IBIZA STYLE |
| 140 | OLD MEETS NEW |

# 04   05   06

## MID-CENTURY

148     FROM MIAMI TO IBIZA

154     URBAN OASIS

160     MOORISH MEETS DISCO

## COLOURFUL

172     THE WORK OF A LIFETIME

184     SEVENTIES CHIC

194     THE BEAT GOES ON

204     A SLICE OF BRAZILIAN MID-CENTURY STYLE

## SOBER

216     BLENDING INTO THE LANDSCAPE

230     LOOKING BACK, LOOKING EAST

236     EARTHY DELIGHTS

246     A NEW TAKE ON MINIMALIST

IBIZA INTERIORS

# INTRODUCTION

Freddy Mercury's birthday party; the hippie movement; sunset at Es Vedrà, shrouded in myth and legend; small secluded coves; the Las Dalias flea market, and, of course, endless parties and the colour white. This all comes to mind when you hear the name Ibiza. The little Balearic island oozes personality and history. Its beaches, mountains and towns have played host to the biggest names in popular culture, but also to anonymous characters simply seeking a slice of island magic. For, despite its diminutive size, there is room for everything on Ibiza. And there are as many different ways to live here as there are reasons to want to experience the island.

In this book, we have brought together 23 interior design projects that perfectly reflect this spirit – wild and free, eclectic and unique, yes, but also intimate and tranquil – and which only a place like Ibiza can offer. Those who inhabit these houses were all looking for different things: to have a place to enjoy their holidays, or to convert their villa into a second home. Some were not able to resist the island's charms and have stayed on to live here permanently. But all have one thing in common – they fell in love with the island and its incontrovertible style.

Whatever the case may be, to give this mix of interior design styles more meaning, the projects have been classified into different categories that aim to find a common thread. 'Cosmopolitan' highlights a style that values aspects such as art, texture and details. 'Eclectic' is an amalgam of projects with an element of eccentricity. 'Mediterranean' style of course had to have a place in the collection, as it reflects the purest and most authentic Ibizan aesthetic. 'Mid-century' recalls the mid-20th century movement and the vintage nostalgia it embodies. The projects featured in 'Colourful' will give readers an extra dose of joy with colour palettes that take on almost psychedelic dimensions. And 'Sober' is the antithesis of what we think of as a typical Ibizan home, providing an incredibly interesting counterpoint.

In short, Ibiza embraces a miscellany of lifestyles, and the aim of this book is to pay tribute to each of them through the prism of its interiors.

# COSMOPOLITAN
# INTERIORS
### ECLECTIC
### MEDITERRANEAN
### MID-CENTURY
### COLOURFUL
### SOBER

# 01

COSMOPOLITAN

# OUT OF THE BLUE

Named after the sky, and offering stunning views of the azure sea, this 200-year-old finca has been remodelled by interior designer Oscar Lucien Ono of Maison Numéro 20 to pay homage to the Mediterranean's blue horizons and stunning sunsets.

Paris-based designer Oscar Lucien Ono is known for his impossibly chic interiors, often featuring deep, bold colours, graphic patterns and dramatic murals. Particular favourite includes electric blues and golden yellows, both of which feature in his redesign for Villa Cielo. Perched on top of one of the Sant Josep hills in Sant Agustí, the historic 300-square-metre farmhouse once belonged to Tony Pike, an icon of the Ibiza party scene and founder of Pikes Hotel who hosted legendary guests including Freddie Mercury and Grace Jones here. It was during this time that it underwent its first renovation, at the hands of the equally renowned architect Rolph Blakstad, also based on the island.

Today, fate has put it in Ono's path, giving it a third reincarnation, with the colours of the sea and the Balearic sunset as the project's central focus. Villa Cielo (meaning 'sky' or 'heaven') is a vibrant tribute to the nature surrounding it. Ono has retained several elements that bear witness to the villa's past, from wooden beams to the sculptural chimney stack that dominates the roof terrace. 'I saw the house's potential very quickly, as well as its exceptional location with a completely unobstructed view of the bay, the town and the greenery,' he explains. 'We had to rethink the space and take out a lot of walls to lose the narrow rooms and make way for surfaces that could breathe.' The entire house is now a huge window onto the outside, with a sliding structure that allows inside and outside to merge in a play of organic architecture and design.

A chandelier in a spectrum of blues takes centre stage in the entrance hall, hanging above a graphic staircase leading to the upper floors and terrace, the latter being a room in its own right. In the living room, original beams add further warmth to a space bathed in sunlight thanks to large windows overlooking the pool and the Sant Josep region beyond. The living/dining room is a cosy and cheerful space with a layout designed for hosting family and friends. A circular sofa by Gallotti & Radice is rounded off with an enormous armchair and glass coffee tables, with a Lelièvre rug in natural hues.

In the entrance hall, a glass chandelier hangs above a graphic floating staircase leading to the upper floors and terrace. A glass balustrade connects the entire house

Villa Cielo is a vibrant tribute to the nature surrounding it. Ono has retained several beams and the exterior structure of the chimney as a kind of sculpture.

The dining room is also a perfect excuse to get together, with a glass table by Silvera and comfortable chairs by Gallotti & Radice. A Bolia lamp illuminates the table in the evenings when the sunlight no longer fills the space. The kitchen, clad in Black Horse marble, reflects light from the large openings in the walls and is completely bespoke. The same can be said of the bedrooms, each given its own personality by using a wide spectrum of blues, with golden accents that emulate the island's sunsets. Art and good taste culminate in a project that values both the traditional and the avant-garde, without detracting from either, nor from the exuberance of the surroundings.

← The rooftop chill-out area comes with stunning views of the bay, with the original chimney stack bringing a sculptural element to the space

COSMOPOLITAN

← ←

Original beams add warmth to the dining area, furnished with a 'Manfred' table by Giuseppe Iasparra for Longhi. The space bathed in sunlight thanks to large windows overlooking the Sant Josep region beyond

←

Here wood plays a leading role in creating a secluded spot overlooking a corner of the garden. The table and two chairs were made in Greece

→

An artwork by Richard Orlinski takes centre stage in the living room, where floor-to-ceiling windows perfectly frame the scenery, leading the eye to the huge tree in the garden

16

COSMOPOLITAN

← Inspired by the island's rays of sunlight and stunning sunsets, the house is peppered with golden accents, including this shimmering wallpaper and stunning 'Ardara' console by Brabbu

COSMOPOLITAN

The entire house is a huge window that opens onto the outside, with a sliding structure that allows inside and outside to merge.

A guest bedroom opens onto the terrace and swimming pool. The white-and-yellow ombré curtains create a dialogue with Ibiza's dazzling sun and surrounding greenery ←

An 'Audrey' armchair by Gallotti & Radice adds curve appeal to the sleek marble bathroom ↓

COSMOPOLITAN

# STARTING FROM SCRATCH

Ali Pittam of Can Can Design and Roberta Jurado of Box3 Interiors worked miracles to inject personality into the blank canvas of a new-build house. The transformation took only six months, but resulted in the totally unrecognisable Can Fructu, now a truly unique and welcoming holiday home.

Ali Pittam, founder and director of Can Can Design, still gets emotional with the satisfaction of a job well done when she recalls the Can Fructu project and everything it entailed: 'As I was driving home, dirty and exhausted, the clients called me to tell me they were completely blown away by what we had done, and that it was better than they ever dreamed it would be. Suddenly, all the adrenaline evaporated, and I had to stop the car at the side of the road and cry with happiness and relief – it had all worked out!' It was far from an easy task for Pittam and her friend and collaborator Roberta Jurado of Box3 Interiores, who were charged with turning the recently bought new-build house into the owners' dream holiday home. It needed absolutely everything, from mattresses and martini glasses to curtains and coffee cups. Their work also included a curved, cantilevered platform to practise yoga, a pétanque court, wine cellar and a gym that had to be 'fully equipped but still beautiful, not just functional'. And all this had to be completed in six months, as the brand-new owners wanted to use the house the first summer after buying it.

The building is a long, low, single-storey house, with a flat roof and beautiful, simple lines, large windows to show off the stunning views, interspersed with the warmth and texture of local stone. Much of the architecture is reminiscent of certain modernist gems in Palm Springs and California. 'As Roberta and I developed the initial interiors concepts, we kept going back to the same phrase: contemporary Mediterranean modernism,' says Pittam. 'This gave us a useful style framework to work within, but it also gave us the confidence to move away from it when we felt it was necessary.' They incorporated furniture, art and accessories from many different eras, multiple countries and continents, with some unique vintage pieces from the 1950s and 1960s that continue the original modernist thread. All of this is set against a backdrop of beautiful, suede-like polished-plaster walls and floors, with imposing full-height hardwood doors.

To bring all this together, it was essential to first get to know the clients and visit some of their other properties. 'It became clear they had a strong preference for a thousand

*The design duo sourced striking pieces of art for the owner, giving this newly built house its own personality*

'As we developed the initial design concepts, we kept going back to the same phrase: contemporary Mediterranean modernism.'

shades of grey. Initially, we were afraid this might be a problem, but, luckily, from the outset they trusted us to guide them. We wanted to move away from the archetypal colours that have been used here on the island for decades: teal, blue, aquamarine; that is, the colours of the sea and the sky. The idea was to root the house in the landscape of the island, so we came up with a scheme centred around a palette of terracotta and ochre, the colours of the rich, living soil and the bright golden stone of Ibiza. 'We set out to inject some fun, joyful personality and character into the home, using strong pops of colour with furniture, bathroom tiles, accessories, and, in particular, some amazing works of art.'

Art and sculpture play an important role in the interior of Can Fructu, as the clients are avid collectors. Some pieces from their other homes were incorporated, but Pittam and Jurado also made a lot of effort to find unique, playful pieces and, above all, to invest in local artists – such as Aline de Laforcade, who created an incredible textured piece in one of the main guest bedrooms, using local sheep wool, Posidonia balls from the beaches and locally produced fibres and fabrics.

→ Instead of using the usual seaside blues and turquoises, the design duo wanted to root the house in the landscape. Their scheme is centred on terracotta tones and features contemporary designs such as these 'Strip' chairs by Massimo Castagna

COSMOPOLITAN

← Although the furniture had to be sourced quickly, the aim was for the home to feel like it had evolved naturally over time. To achieve this, contemporary European and South American designer items have been interspersed with vintage pieces

→ A pair of 'Stud' bar stools by Diesel Living with Moroso complement the marble and wood kitchen island

COSMOPOLITAN

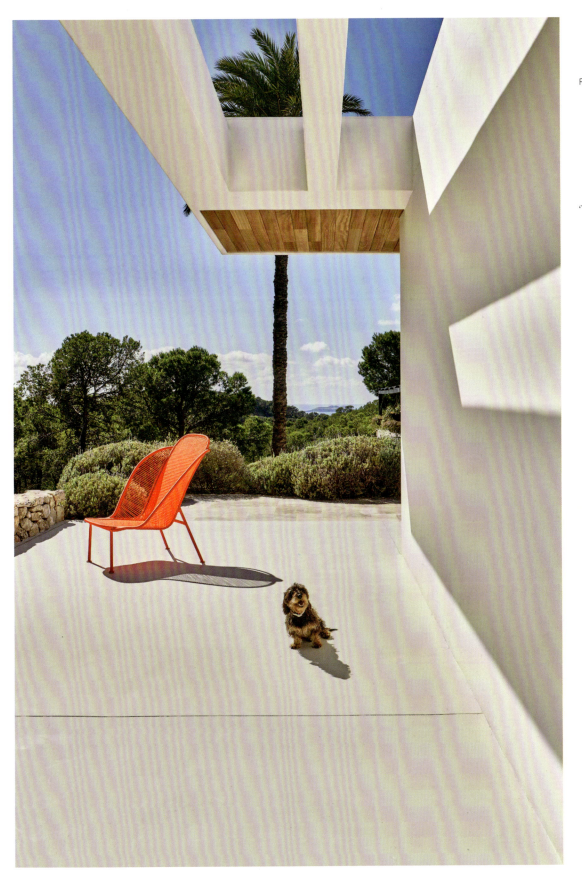

→
A Christian Rosa painting hangs in the main bedroom

→ →
A bedroom furnished with the 'Carve 07' chair by Paola Navone, an artwork by British artist Ben Eine, and the iconic 1970s 'Togo' sofa by Michel Ducaroy for Ligne Roset

←
The low, single-storey house comes with a pristine white exterior – the best colour to keep the house cool while also contrasting with the green surroundings

COSMOPOLITAN

Art and sculpture play an important role in the interior of Can Fructu, as the clients are avid collectors.

The curved, cantilevered yoga platform and cedar hot tub are surrounded by nature ←

Beautiful, suede-like polished plaster walls and floor form a textured backdrop ↓

↑ Summer hats and straw bags bring a touch of the beachside to this bathroom, finished in microcement and home to a bright red 'Zig Zag' stool by Polspotten

Lots of wood, a bar area and comfortable sofas; another key element in this project was to create a relaxing space in which to enjoy the outside space and savour the sunset

COSMOPOLITAN

# ADAPT AND THRIVE

Having spent decades planning the Can Arabí villa, architect Jaime Romano had to rethink the whole project when new owners came on board. Incorporating both the original vision and softer, more classical additions, the result is greater than the sum of its parts.

Beyond its refined interior design, wonderful combination of different kinds of local stone, and fine finishes, this project, Can Arabí, was 'one of those lessons in humility that architecture teaches you,' according to Jaime Romano, founder and owner of Romano Architects design studio, which led the new-build. 'It was a very complicated project, and a very long one,' he explains. 'It took ten years to develop, ten years to get planning permission. When we finally got it, the German couple who had hired us for the project were already 75 years old, and they decided to sell the property with the plans. It was bought by a German couple in their fifties, who wanted to give it a more classical feel, especially in terms of its external appearance. It's important to bear in mind that this was a project with very distinct, very gestural lines, determined by the topography itself, its location in a clearing in the forest, and the orientation of the views.' Ultimately, it was a very modern project, and one which didn't marry up with the new family's imagined concept.

'I remember that first meeting with my second clients perfectly. I suddenly found myself face to face with a totally different vision for the house. And my ego found itself in a kind of battle with the idea I had developed over the course of ten years, by that point almost an archaeological projection since, for me, the project was fossilized in my mind. And all of a sudden I found I had to dismantle it to be able to incorporate this softer, more Mediterranean vision, with references to Mallorcan architecture, a vernacular which clearly favours stone. And I soon had to decide whether to give up the project and stay true to my original idea, or, with that sense of humility and care, to adapt.'

Obviously, Romano chose the latter: 'Experience had made me mature as an architect over the previous ten years. And, as a result, there was this tension between my original vision based on the first brief, and all the work involved in adapting it to incorporate these more classical, ancient elements.' This was ultimately achieved using a combination of stone from different quarries, pergolas with climbing plants – an element proposed by the studio, with a very light and open

The owners' dream was to give their house a Mediterranean air. The studio fulfilled this by combining stones from different quarries and drawing on references to Mallorcan architecture

It was a long and complicated project, as it took ten years for planning permission to be granted. And then it changed hands.

metal structure which simply invites the plants to form a cover – as well as straw baskets, typical of Mediterranean vernacular architecture. 'Once we had established this classic Mediterranean backdrop with sandstone and this symbiosis between architecture and climbing plants, these outside spaces covered with baskets, we then created a very refined interior – very modern, but at the same time alive with colour.' The base tones and fine materials give a playful nod to colour and allow a clever mix of contemporary details with more artisan-style pieces, like the ultramarine blue Botteganove tiles in the dining room, paying tribute to the Mediterranean Sea beyond.

With the clients wanting to spend as much time as possible outside, much attention was given to the outdoor decor. The interior appears as an extension of it, and not the other way around as is often the case. Rugs delineate spaces and add warmth; fireplaces partition rooms; wood and design pieces come together to form a house that almost didn't happen, but which, thanks to a good decision and careful adaptation, ended up being wonderful.

→ Above all, the villa was built to enjoy the outdoor area. Hence the cosy seating arrangement under the pergolas and the shading vegetation, all arranged to share moments

⬅

The main living room is furnished with a 'Campiello' sofa by Antonio Citterio for Flexform, with a fish cushion by J-Line; a pair of 'PK22' armchairs by Poul Kjærholm for Fritz Hansen, and table and glass chess set from local vintage boutique Mon Château en Espagne

➡

Designed by Box3 Ibiza, the kitchen features built-in cabinetry by Poliform in walnut wood with stainless-steel handles. The worktops are bush-hammered San Vicente stone, while the bar stools are from Polspotten

COSMOPOLITAN

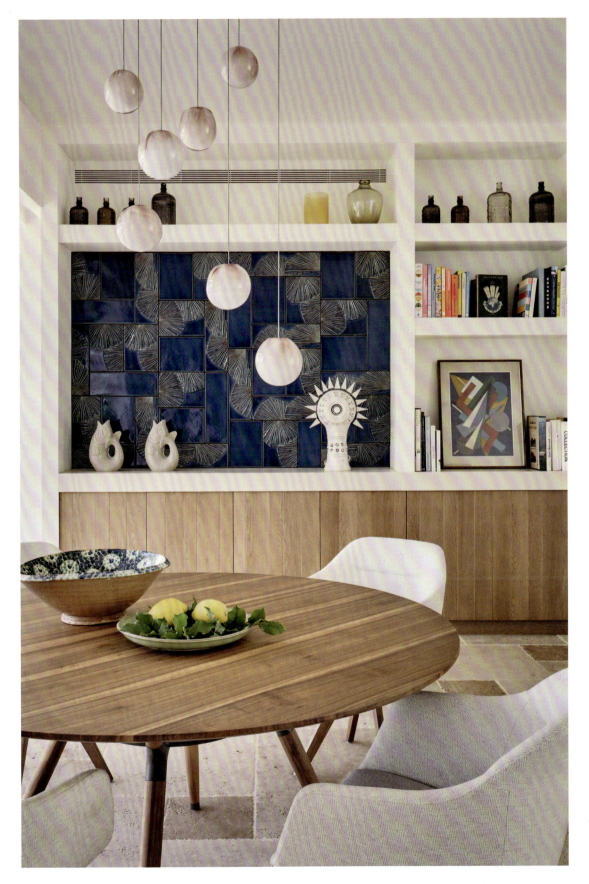

A chandelier by Omer Arbel for Bocci hangs in the dining area, where a 'X2' table made by Mobimex is paired with 'Cara' chairs by Bielefelder Werkstätten and tiles by Botteganove

The studio settled on a very refined, modern interior decor, at the same time vibrant with colour and playing with artisan elements.

The character of the house is defined from the very entrance, where we are welcomed by a Mares stone, natural wood panelling, lush vegetation and the stone fireplace in the background

In the living room we find a Mademoiselle chair from the 1960s by Scandinavian designer Ilmari Tapiovaara with sheepskin, a plexiglass chess set and a pair of Pk22 chairs in black leather by designer Poul Kjaerholm

→ The white walls and traditional flagstone floors of this bedroom are complemented by 1950s-inspired table lights, a sheepskin rug and abstract artworks

COSMOPOLITAN

←
The perfect indoor/ outdoor combination is created in the bedroom with its own private terrace. And the classic esparto blinds, a very traditional method of sun protection, make for the perfect Mediterranean touch

45

↑
The colour of the bedspread keeps in tone with the rest of the serene elements in the bedroom, while the pompons add a touch of playfulness to the paired-back space

The wall is finished with Salvatori's Pietra d'Avola Plissé stone. The bespoke oak wall-hung dressing table is a real eye-catcher

COSMOPOLITAN

# COOL, CALM AND COLLECTED

TG-Studio's design for Can Bikini focuses on the international, relaxed style it believes best reflects Ibiza. Here, the relationship between the inside and outside spaces is so fluid it makes the villa appear even more spacious.

Planning restrictions prohibited the expansion of Can Bikini building, but this was a blessing in disguise, as it allowed TG-Studio to bring the beauty of its rural surroundings into the heart of this stunning villa. The designers were given free rein on the interiors, which were in dire need of a facelift, by the owners – UK property developers – who use the villa for family holidays and rent it to friends and acquaintances when away.

The three-bedroom property is nestled in the rich pine forests of the north of Ibiza, and is surrounded by two hectares of lush gardens, with two additional houses providing two more bedrooms with en-suite bathrooms, as well as a self-contained casita. The main house consists of a large living room, with 4-metre-high ceilings and sliding glass doors that double the size of the space in summer; a dining room and an open-plan kitchen diner. There are two master bedrooms on this floor, both with en-suite bathrooms, and another bedroom with a shower and roof terrace on the first floor. The gardens include a large open-air swimming pool and a summer house to relax in, with chill-out zone and bar, as well as an outdoor gym and yoga deck.

TG-Studio took various measures to take full advantage of the great bones of the place. The first thing was to demolish the kitchen and install a state-of-the-art Doca kitchen complete with Gaggenau appliances, flamed black granite worktops, grey mirrored splashback and white-painted oak doors. A new wood-burning fireplace was installed with flamed granite base and black steel surround; a structure which also houses a 70-inch television, surround sound system and a new double-height towel store. This made it possible to incorporate the bread oven alcove into the main room, introducing a circular skylight and four different-shaped windows with yellow stained glass that creates a spacious chill-out nook. In the evening the windows give off a warm glow, standing out against the stone of the facade. The entire natural stone floor was sanded and sealed, and the house was repainted

*The alcove that once housed the bread oven has been opened up to create a fantastic reading nook in the main living room. Finished in black and white, the whole space gives off the sense of tranquillity the owners were looking for*

# The house itself was fabulous but the interior had become outdated and needed modernisation.

← The living room boasts a new fireplace with flamed granite base and black steel surround. The chimney breast also houses a 70-inch television, surround sound system and a new double-height towel store

→ The state-of-the-art Doca kitchen comes complete with Gaggenau appliances, flamed black granite worktops, a grey mirrored splashback and white-painted oak doors. The 'Masters' stools are by Philippe Starck and Eugeni Quitllet for Kartell

and fully furnished by TG-Studio. 'As all the finishes and colours are kept in the Ibizan cool white,' explains Thomas Griem, head of TG-Studio, 'colour and texture were key when choosing the furniture, to create that London cool hits Ibiza feel.'

Outside, a cabin was imported directly from Bali, which the garden building is named after, and which boasts an incredible open-air bathroom. TG-Studio added furniture to complement the scheme, including Andrew Martin's Bobbili Stool wooden side tables and birdcage desk lamp. 'The pool house was extended and rearranged to accommodate a large bar with built-in refrigerators, a grill and a wood-fired pizza oven,' the studio adds. TG-Studio designed the furniture, which was then manufactured and upholstered in Holly Hunt fabrics by local contractors.

↑
A classic wishbone chair in one of the bedrooms. The walls are all in a cool Ibizan white colour, while natural material and texture were key when choosing the furniture

COSMOPOLITAN

← The monochrome look continues in this bathroom with a striking dark bathtub

COSMOPOLITAN
**ECLECTIC
INTERIORS**
MEDITERRANEAN
MID-CENTURY
COLOURFUL
SOBER

ECLECTIC

# A PLACE OF ONE'S OWN

Francesca Munizaga and Alonso Colmenares are the proud owners of this farmhouse dating back to 1890. Thanks to their careful remodelling, the creative pair has brought in their unique personal style without losing the essence of the historic building.

With twins on the way and living in a one-bedroom apartment Francesca Munizaga and Alonso Colmenares, founders of local sustainable florist The Flower Studio, were already facing a difficult scenario when they took over this old, 200-square-metre farmhouse with stables and 8 hectares of land. Alonso had to take a break from his day job and hire a bigger team so that the house would be ready when the babies arrived. It's therefore hardly surprising that this became such a personal project, which perfectly defines its owners and, what's more, one that has respected the very essence of this old Ibizan house.

The layout is very simple, consisting of a living room, kitchen, dining room, guest bedroom with en-suite bathroom and children's room, all on the ground floor. Upstairs is the master bedroom, which also has an en-suite bathroom. The charm of this villa is in the detail, the decor and the way the couple has made it their own, keeping in mind how basic the original facilities were. 'Our aim was to bring it to life as a family home, with a view to one day opening a rural hotel,' Francesca says. 'We moved two days before our due date and didn't even have a kitchen, so I bought a fridge, toaster and kettle and that's how we survived at first.'

There is not a single element that does not come with a special memory. 'Most of the things here have a little story behind them; they're pieces we found in markets all over the world, but primarily the local Sant Jordi market and a nearby auction house in Santa Gertrudis called Casi Todo, meaning "almost everything"; we found some real gems on this island,' continues Francesca. 'It has to be said that during the renovation we didn't touch the living room. It had a beautiful atmosphere, and the ceilings were high for an old Ibizan house, but we needed somewhere to put all our little treasures, so we built a floor-to-ceiling bookcase, and we're constantly moving things around.'

Francesca and Alonso firmly believe that what is useless to some people might be valuable to others, so they decided to take a trip to southern Spain to look around demolition sites. 'We came across some beautiful old tiles,

*The farmhouse dates back to 1890 and features a shady terrace with a reclaimed brick floors and vintage finds*

'Most of the things here have a little story behind them; they're pieces that are important and beautiful to us.'

A smooth white facade, simple benches with striped cushions and aquamarine doors create a perfectly symmetric entrance

including the ones in the kitchen and guest bathroom, and we found the star of the kitchen: the old, traditional raw stone sink. We also discovered the old brick tiles on the terrace and around the pool, which are fabulous, and the children's bathtub... We have so many things that we find beautiful – furniture and ornaments that we adore. We always bring something back from our travels.' As well as reclamation yards, they scour second-hand shops for classic pieces, and galleries for contemporary artworks: 'We like old things, things with patina, but we do have some design pieces too, like the Eames chairs, the Noguchi table, the 'Ball' chair by Eero Aarnio. We have a lot of works by Sandoval, a very talented, very fun Venezuelan artist based in Madrid. We also collect artists who work on the island, like Grillo Demo. We love his objects and paintings.'

Everything is so 'them' that if you ask them to define their style, they do so with 'US' in capital letters, because they simply put together all the things they love without following any particular rule; all that matters is that things mean something to them. They are eclectic and not especially minimalist, at least not inside. The outside space is quite the opposite: peaceful, organic and regenerative, respectful of the colours of nature. There is a huge table built around a carob tree beside the pool – designed for the fun of family life, and with the idea of eventually converting this place into a rustic hotel.

The house had high ceilings for an old Ibizan house, but the owners needed somewhere to put all their little treasures, so they built a floor-to-ceiling unit with shelves of various shapes and sizes, allowing them to change the display regularly

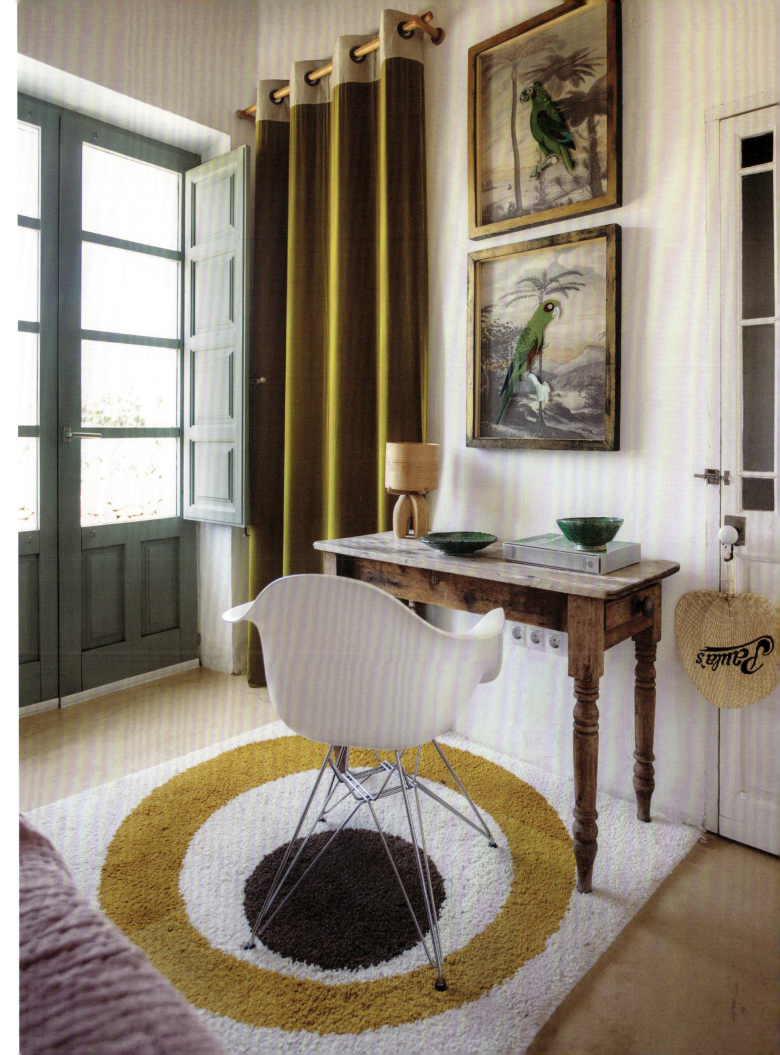

⬅︎⬅︎ The original wooden ceiling was kept to give the space the rustic feel they were looking for. The rest of the living room is filled with mid-century-style furniture and vintage pieces such as a Noguchi coffee table and egg chair

⬅︎ Most of the things here have a little story behind them; they're pieces that were found in markets all over the world, but primarily the local Sant Jordi market and a nearby auction house in Santa Gertrudis called Casi Todo, meaning 'almost everything'

➡︎ A wonderful encaustic cement-tile floor defines the kitchen-diner space, which combines raw stone walls with white lacquered units

ECLECTIC

Fierce advocates of the concept of recycling, the owners found beautiful antique tiles and the centrepiece, an old, traditional raw stone sink, on reclamation yards

ECLECTIC

**Fierce advocates of the concept of recycling, Francesca and Alonso believe that what is useless to some people might be valuable to others.**

Warm textures and ochre hues envelop the master bedroom, with a 'Peacock' rattan chair taking pride of place by the windows ←

The eclectic yet functional cloakroom ↓

→ Graphic blue-and-white floor tiles are paired with raw stone in the bathroom

ECLECTIC

Dramatic red wall tiles complete the look, contrasting radically with the floor

ECLECTIC

# A CAREFULLY CRAFTED CASA

This striking contemporary home was made to measure by Barcelona's Alfons & Damián studio for its vegan and dog-loving owners. An ode to craftmanship and design, the project features no material derived from animals and is perfectly adapted to our four-legged friends' needs.

The starting point for this project was a brand-new house with simple finishes that lacked personality. The brief given to the Alfons & Damián design studio was to adapt it to the needs of the clients and make it more characterful. There were some essentials that had to be taken into account: for example, a cinema room and an outside space just as comfortable as the inside, with a kitchen, dining room and living room. But encompassing all of this was the fact that the owners are vegans and dog lovers: 'The house reflects an animal-free project, where the furniture could not derive from animals, and also had to be dog friendly,' say its designers Alfons Tost and Damián Sánchez.

The 490 square metres are distributed over two storeys, comprising a ground-floor entrance hall, main living room, kitchen, terrace with pergola, cinema room, patio and three suites, as well as a first-floor master bedroom. 'The bathrooms and kitchen were redistributed and remodelled. The house had a large fourth suite on the ground floor, which we transformed into a cinema room. We also connected the entire daytime area with the outside, giving the house total freedom to communicate from inside to outside, where two separate guest suites were built in the middle of the garden.'

To fulfil the brief, materials such as wood, stucco, brass, iron and natural fibres were chosen. Most of the furniture follows simple, linear shapes in natural materials like wood, raffia, linen and cotton. Several iconic pieces were added, such as the red 'Macao' table by François Champsaur for Pouenat, and the Warren Platner chairs from Knoll.

This whole environment is embraced by the natural light that flows into the house, which is really quite intense, as it is surrounded by large glass doors and windows which connect with the entire outside area of the garden. The lighting was designed to be warm and enveloping, establishing several specific light sources for each area, combined with pendant, table, floor and wall lights. 'We prefer to use auxiliary lighting that gives gentle illumination, rather than having ambient lighting which can detract from the atmosphere of a space,'

In the entrance hall, a black floating staircase, bold artwork, and a lantern by Miguel Milá for Santa & Cole perched on a rustic wooden bench announce the villa's pared-back style

**The entire daytime area is now connected with the outside, giving the house total freedom to communicate from inside to outside.**

explain Alfons and Damián. 'When it came to colours, we mixed the existing natural stone walls with soft hues and white tones throughout the house. Touches of black and red were used in the decor.'

The black floating staircase, which seems to hover in the space, draws the eye in. This can also be said of the sliding shutters, reminiscent of barn doors, finished in wood and hung from wrought black iron – a traditional way of avoiding the need for blinds. And although the interior tends to feature more sophisticated lines, the outside aspires to be more in tune with the nature that surrounds it. This starts with the earthy, neutral colours with flashes of red to tie in with the interior, and ends with the simplicity of its finishes, and the large, open spaces in which to enjoy the company of humans and, of course, animals. It is, as the studio itself describes it, 'a space where nature and the artisan world so typical of the island merge with the luxury of wellbeing'. The combination of natural elements is the secret to a welcoming home that respects the environment.

→ The kitchen appliances are hidden behind bespoke wooden cabinets, while the large island is long enough to provide a bar to sit and eat at. Three open shelves display the items used most regularly

ECLECTIC

The lighting was designed to be warm and enveloping, establishing several specific light sources for each area.

← The large living room comes with exposed beams, a pair of red Warren Platner chairs from Knoll and a tree root centrepiece above the fireplace

↓ The wood cladding in the kitchen lends warmth to the overall feel

→ Black is used to great effect in this project, such as in the dining area, featuring 'Huma' armchairs by Expormim

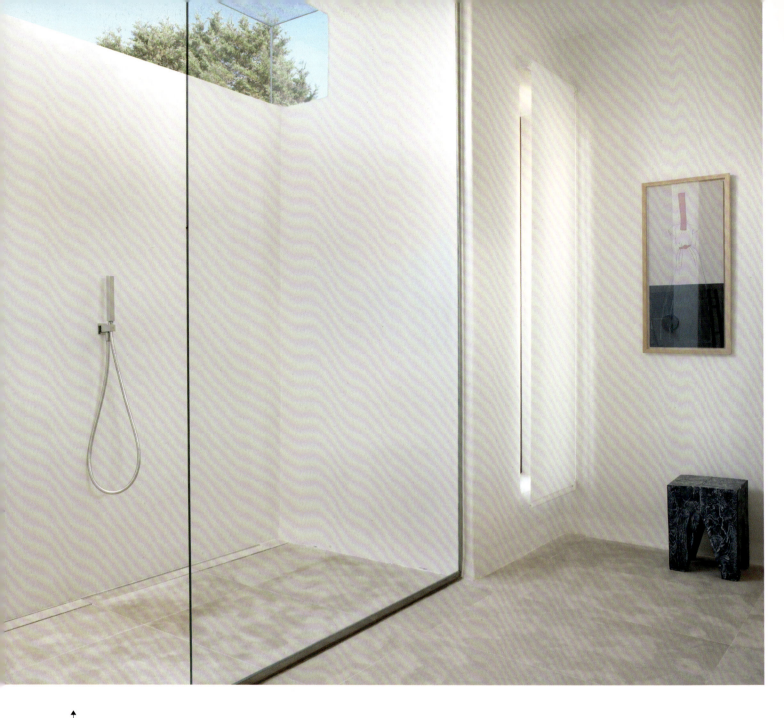

↑
A large overhead lightwell in the indoor shower maximises natural light and creates connection with the outside space

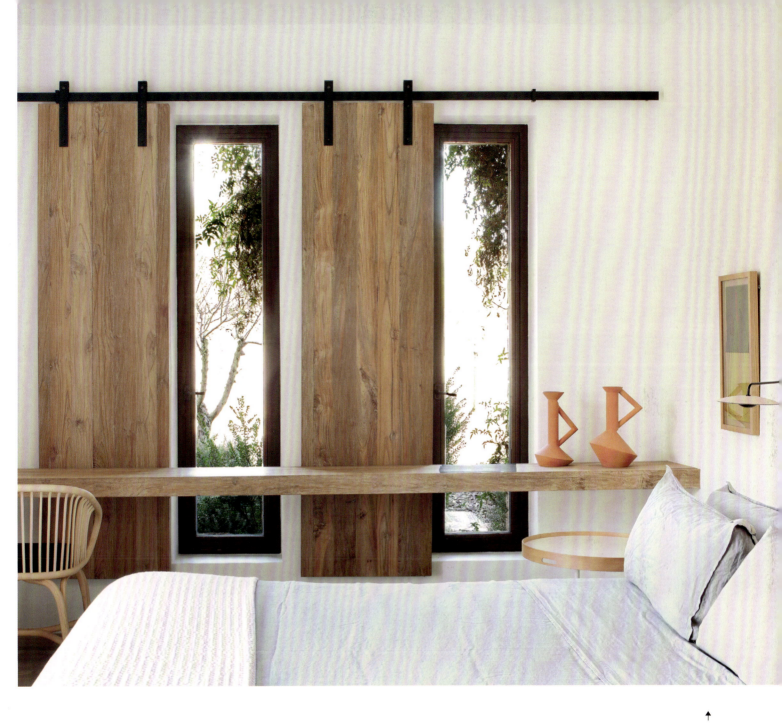

↑
Hung from wrought-iron runners, the eye-catching sliding wooden shutters are reminiscent of barn doors and offer an rustic alternative to blinds

81

ECLECTIC

# BETWEEN TWO SEAS

Situated within the Cala Carbó–Cala d'Hort Natural Park, Villa Umaya boasts stunning views out over two stretches of coastline. Ksar Living design studio capitalised on this unique seafront setting, resulting in a truly special home.

Design, decoration and style come together in such a way in this project that the newly built Villa Umaya feels homely yet modern, relaxed yet luxurious, cosy yet minimalist, as if it has been this way for ever. Ksar Living's design is all about celebrating the villa's special location within the Cala Carbó–Cala d'Hort nature reserve. The area is also known as 'Between Two Seas', because it enjoys spectacular views of the south-west coast and the magical rock of Es Vedrà on one side, and on the other the island's Mediterranean west coast. Capitalising on this setting, as well as creating as much light as possible, and establishing a style that is the perfect mix of modern and minimalist, were the key objectives Ksar Living's Jaime Serra and Yvonne Sophie Hulst from Es Vedrà Bay Villas set out to achieve.

The villa measures 516 square metres and sits within a 1,320 square-metre plot. It comprises a basement with three bedrooms complete with en-suite bathrooms; a ground floor with a large living room and pool, spacious kitchen and bedroom with en-suite bathroom; and finally the first floor, with a bedroom and en-suite bathroom, leading out onto a large terrace. How best to achieve the desired style while at the same time bringing in the environment so that it becomes an element in its own right within the project? Ksar Living found the answer: 'In this project we used a great deal of natural stone, cement finishes, wooden panelling, reclaimed wood, and eclectic and exotic decor. Several of the walls have been clad with dark-grey lava stone. Every aspect of the development was meticulously planned to ensure efficiency, and carefully overseen to guarantee the highest possible standards, impeccable finishes and materials, and exceptional craftsmanship.'

Of all the solutions included in the design, the staircase is without doubt one of the most striking. 'The impressive staircase, crafted with a combination of different kinds of natural stone and lots of wooden panels, is a very pivotal piece in the house,' explain the designers. 'Not only for its appearance, but also because it leads

*Capitalising on the spectacular views, as well as creating as much light as possible and establishing a style that is the perfect mix of modern and minimalist, were KsaR Living's key objectives*

'In this project we used a great deal of natural stone, cement finishes, wooden panelling, reclaimed wood, and eclectic and exotic decor.'

to the bedroom on the top floor, which in turn connects with the huge rooftop terrace, with its stunning 360-degree vistas, where you can admire the magical sunset.' As with the other bedrooms, the views here look out towards Es Vedrà.

Another of the villa's defining characteristics is that, in the quest for natural light, the studio decided to install huge sliding doors on every side. This solution also means that the surroundings – the plot, garden and pool – all form an intrinsic part of the house, as though they constitute another layer of decoration. Choosing the right colours is always key to creating the desired effect. In this case, the interior design studio settled on a very natural and minimalist colour spectrum; a palette that favours neutral tones, bringing in a touch of colour through the use of cushions, rugs and other textiles.

'Interior design isn't just a job or a process for us; it's a feeling. We might be global nomads, but at the end of the day there's no place like home.' Never a truer word spoken.

→ As you step out of the living room you encounter the infinity pool, a true delight with a backdrop of lush scenery that seems almost to merge into the surroundings

ECLECTIC

'The impressive staircase, crafted with a combination of different kinds of natural stone and lots of wooden panels, is a very pivotal piece in the house.'

The finca sits within the Cala Carbó-Cala d'Hort Natural Park, with spectacular views of the sea along the south-west coast and the magical rock of Es Vedrà, and on the other side the Mediterranean west coast of the island

The project used a great deal of cement finishes, wooden panelling and reclaimed wood, and the resulting decor is both eclectic and exotic

Several interior walls are clad with dark-grey lava stone

↑
The first-floor bedroom with en-suite bathroom leads out onto a large terrace planted with palm trees

ECLECTIC

← The free-standing bathtub, also finished in grey stone, looks out over the garden

COSMOPOLITAN
ECLECTIC
**MEDITERRANEAN
INTERIORS**
MID-CENTURY
COLOURFUL
SOBER

03

MEDITERRANEAN

# HOME AT LAST

Having viewed over 80 houses, fashion CEO Sarah Crook was about to give up her search when she finally stumbled on The One. She turned interior designer and project manager to renovate it, in a truly impressive debut.

'This house is at the heart of the island, near Santa Gertrudis, and yet at the same time it is completely isolated,' says Sarah Crook of her villa. The fashion company director couldn't be happier about her new home, though she had been on the verge of throwing in the towel before she found it: 'I had seen more than 80 houses in just under two years,' she explains. 'Just when I felt like giving up, I went to see five villas with a new agent. Mine was the last one, and I had already given it a resounding no when I saw the pictures, as it was nothing like what I'd imagined. The house was built in the 1980s by two German owners and had a central tower topped with a crown, and no front door. It was the opposite of my dream house, but I could immediately see the potential the house would have once it was renovated.'

Sarah knew from the outset what she wanted to achieve, and despite not being a professional developer (her first foray as an interior designer was in this very place), she was quick when it came to making decisions: 'I saw potential straight away as I walked around the house. I completely remodelled the whole house, but without adding any square footage or touching the structure. There was a large garage and storage space to one side that I knew would make a great kitchen and living space, which would also allow me to have a large entrance hall to make the most of the views. Upstairs, I built an outdoor bathroom off the master bedroom and remodelled the existing family bathroom. Downstairs, I converted the original kitchen into a private bathroom next to the new bedroom that overlooks the pool and garden. This area has amazing views and it's one of my favourite rooms. The house now has two very separate living areas; the kitchen that opens onto a new terrace, which in turn leads out onto a part of the garden that was completely overgrown; and the original living room, which is really snug in winter and wonderful to read in.' Sarah also turned the walls into a textured blank canvas and installed iron-framed glass doors and windows.

Inside, a natural and textured palette was used, with wicker baskets, pale walls and rugs, and a 1950s rattan floor lamp

95

'I love flea markets, vintage fairs, French antiques and, more than anything else, chairs.'

With this project, she was looking to recreate that sense of balance that exists on the island; so full of life in summer and so calm and cosy on winter days. She therefore settled on a natural and textured colour palette, while, in terms of materials, wood, wicker, bamboo, cement and natural plaster take centre stage, with splashes of colour appearing through objects, ceramics and paintings. 'With the exception of the herringbone terracotta tiles in the bathroom, I wanted the flooring to be uniform throughout the entire house, maintaining the sense of space and light. All the walls are finished in a simple, raw plaster that gives a natural, textured finish as opposed to paint or colour.' Pieces of furniture, drawn from a mixture of countries and exotic tastes, highlight Sarah's unique style. 'I love flea markets, vintage fairs, French antiques. I'm completely obsessed with chairs and continue to collect them for no reason. I adore mid-century designs from the 1960s and 1970s, especially wicker and rattan, as well as selected African pieces I've collected on various trips.' It was well worth the wait, and now there's nothing Sarah loves more than watching the sunrise in her bedroom as she indulges in a 'slow and lazy' breakfast.

→ The large kitchen cum dining room was carved out of an existing large garage and storage space. Handmade tableware in cool celadon add a touch of colour to this zen space

MEDITERRANEAN

← The original living room has been preserved and is a snug haven in the winter months – the perfect spot for quiet reading

→ A 'Bird of Paradise' rattan chair by Raj Tent Club and 'Birdy' wall lamps by Northern stand out against a backdrop of simple, raw-plaster walls

MEDITERRANEAN

← A little outdoor lounge with fireplace, built-in benches and a sculptural woven cactus: all you need to enjoy the peaceful side of Ibizan life

MEDITERRANEAN

'I changed all the floors and walls to create a textured blank canvas that I could work with, and installed iron-framed glass doors and windows.'

The wooden veranda, table and benches are paired with rattan lamps and cushions, exposed stone walls and lush vegetation ←

A rare splash colour in the form of a graphic artwork by Adam Bridgland adds a new dimension to a corner that could have been overlooked ↓

ECLECTIC

→ A concealed staircase featuring a traditional niche leads to the light-soaked upper floor

ECLECTIC

← A new bedroom on the ground floor comes with an built-in plaster four-poster bed and French doors leading out onto the pool and garden

MEDITERRANEAN

# A SENSE OF CRAFT

The owner of this stunning villa in Ibiza's old town has chosen to update her 1970s house by using traditional flagstone floors and dressing the space with beautifully crafted pieces by local artisans.

The founder of Habitat Property in Hong Kong, with over 18 years' experience of finding houses for other people, developer Victoria Allan was delighted to find this gem of a property (it is literally called 'La Joya', the jewel) in Ibiza. 'I was very involved in the design process and knew exactly how I wanted the house to look. I had a very different aesthetic in mind and wanted to incorporate local materials wherever I could,' explains Victoria, who worked with Dutch architects Ibiza Interiors and interior designer Hadrien Breitenach to transform the two-bedroom villa, which had not been updated since it was built in the early 1970s.

Victoria radically transformed the 200-square-metre property, which came with a separate guesthouse: 'We opened up the house, creating three bedrooms by moving the kitchen into the living room and making it open-plan. The master bedroom was created by combining the original kitchen, storage room, laundry room and guest bathroom. We converted the guesthouse into a kids' bunkroom and an entertainment room with TV. We also made the windows bigger to take advantage of the views, re-landscaped all the gardens and created several outdoor living spaces, including a kitchen with barbeque and pizza oven. All the floors were laid with local Ibizan stone, and we used as many local products and artisans as possible.' The flagstones were inspired by those found in Dalt Vila, the upper part of the historic centre of Ibiza Town, a UNESCO World Heritage Site since 1999.

Inside, the colour palette is based on an original artwork: 'The main house is influenced by an amazing green painting by Tanya Ling. This green set the tone for the rest of the house, and I even managed to source matching vintage 1950s Italian chairs in the same colour. We had all the rugs made bespoke and found other vintage pieces to give the space a unique feel.' Victoria also found some fantastic rattan lampshades by Atelier Vime, and tried to keep the finishes minimal, both inside and out. Swirling greens and brick-red terracotta hues breathe life into the home and flow naturally into the lush hills and cliffs among which the house is nestled.

The sizeable plot is big enough to house two new outdoor dining areas, an outdoor kitchen and a spacious poolside terrace

# 'All the floors were laid with local Ibizan stone, and we used as many local products and artisans as possible.'

To fully enjoy Ibiza's sun-drenched lifestyle, Victoria created several spaces for alfresco dining and entertaining. 'I also spent a lot of time thinking about landscaping the garden to make it feel like part of the house, connecting the inside with the outside and vice versa.' Given the sizeable plot that the villa sits within, Victoria was able to create two separate dining areas, an outdoor kitchen complete with a wood-fired pizza oven and barbeque area, and a spacious poolside terrace. Arnaud Casaus, a landscape gardener from Paris, worked with Victoria to retain as many indigenous plants as possible and further integrate the property with its natural environment.

'I adore Ibiza and its unique atmosphere,' says Victoria. 'Islanders can have the best of both worlds; choosing whether to take advantage of the laid-back beach resorts or the buzzing nightlife.'

→ During the renovation, all the gardens were re-landscaped and several outdoor living spaces were developed, including a fully equipped kitchen with barbeque and pizza oven

MEDITERRANEAN

'The main house is influenced by a green painting by Tanya Ling, and this colour set the tone for the rest of the house.'

Vintage 1950s Italian chairs in the dining room and kitchen

The cosy lounge, with a local Ibizan flagstone floor, a suspended woodburning stove and an 1950s armchair by Adrien Audoux and Frida Minet

The kitchen was moved into the living room to create a large open-plan space. Solid wood bar stools and a vintage bamboo and rattan bar car complement the wooden cabinets and marble counters

MEDITERRANEAN

←
An amazing painting by Tanya Ling, with its suggestion of organic growth, sets the tone for the rest of the house. The stunning chandelier is by Atelier Vime

→
An outdoor shower continues the flow between inside and outside. It features a stunning dry-stone wall and a 1960s bamboo and rattan stool by Franco Albini

MEDITERRANEAN

← Working with Parisian landscape gardener Arnaud Casaus, the owner retained as many indigenous plants as possible

MEDITERRANEAN

# THE GREAT OUTDOORS

Having fallen in love with the patio of this beautiful finca in Cala Carbó, its creative owners set out to turn the outside spaces into a series of welcoming exterior rooms.

'It is the outside spaces, designed as rooms in their own right, which give the villa its magic. This, and the stunning views out over the rock of Es Vedrà. All this as a whole imbues the house with a serene, otherworldly energy,' says its owners, fashion creative Deborah Brett and filmmaker Tom Edmunds, who enlisted the help of John Broekman of Blue Pearl to shape this 480-square-metre finca in Cala Carbó. Built in the 1980s, it had originally a very different style, with railings, orange window frames and even gravelled gardens and battlements on the walls. All of this disappeared in favour of a clean, simple exterior aesthetic that came together in harmony with the materials.

'We wanted to reflect the landscape in the textures we used in the building elements, and create different areas where guests could take time out to relax by themselves,' explain the owners. To this end, both the main building and the guesthouse were renovated to create three bedrooms, three bathrooms, a kitchen and living room in the former, and in the latter, two bedrooms, two bathrooms, a table tennis area with a special cut-flower garden. But if there is one thing that was fully maximised, it has to be all the outside space. 'It was essential to have lots of different areas to relax in various parts of the outside space, so that you could escape if it got too hot. We created simple corners to sit with plush pillows, areas with swivel chairs to read and relax. We built a wooden treehouse and climbing play area for the kids, including a fireman's pole, slide and lookout tower. We also have a small orchard and vegetable garden to grow our own produce. An area for me to do pottery outside, also doubles up as a yoga space. And then there is the pool house, which has its own kitchen.'

That quest for tranquillity, so typical of Ibiza, is reflected in the materials that were used to decorate, from sharp stone to rope and leather, reclaimed, untreated wood as well as the wash of indigo colours that reflect the Mediterranean Sea. 'We used local juniper wood on the underside of the porches which lend a warm, rustic feel to the building. They are large-scale and untreated. We wanted their natural beauty to shine through, and not be masked with

The owners restored the antique wooden gates that open onto a large, tiled patio area

119

'We wanted to reflect the landscape with the textures we used in the building elements, and create several different zones.'

→ → The natural palette and materials are complemented by a wash of indigo colours that reflect the Mediterranean Sea, appearing in pieces such as a Berber rug, the powder-blue woodwork and a painting by Tanya Ling. The white ceramic vase in one of the owner's creations

varnish. For the patio, we used three different patterns of blue-and-white tiles from Mosaic Factory, a Spanish tile company. The first is a pattern of Ipanema waves, which is really dynamic and bold, in the main patio area. Then we used a smaller one with a star design in the dining room and an eye pattern in our outdoor lounge/cinema area.'

'As a potter,' Deborah enthuses, 'I'm obsessed with tiles. It was important for me to use different colours and tiles in every room, from the blue ombré in the two guest bathrooms, to the thick, wavy ones in the kitchen and the reclaimed Provence terracotta tiles in the living room. We also loved using local artisans for the different textures on the cabinet doors – from the woven sisal panels on the guest bedroom doors to the master bedroom's bamboo panels and rope headboard. Every piece is unique.' One-off pieces like the contemporary portraits by the photographer Shawna Ankenbrandt, the 1960s ceramic vases and the antique wooden armoire that belonged to Deborah's mother come together to establish an interior style with masses of personality.

→ The patio features 'Ipanema' blue-and-white tiles from Spanish tile company Mosaic Factory. As a potter, the tiles were a very important element for the owner, and were therefore given much thought

MEDITERRANEAN

From the woven sisal panels on the guest bedroom doors to the master bedroom's bamboo panels and rope headboard, every piece is unique.

The kitchen bar, with a black slate countertop, reclaimed timber cupboards, HZI seagrass pendant lights, and wooden stools from Mona Market in Paris ←←

Large daybeds upholstered in Designers Guild fabric are set up on the travertine poolside terrace ←

The herringbone floor is a key feature that runs throughout much of the house ↓

MEDITERRANEAN

→ The wooden ceiling of the sheltered outdoor lounge is made of sun-dried tree trunks

MEDITERRANEAN

A bespoke rope headboard, 'Dandelion' floor tiles from Marrakech Design, Fermoie cushions and yellow linen throw by Once Milano all feature in the master bedroom

→ A free-standing bathtub looks more like a hemp basket than a bathtub. Everything has been designed to flow as naturally as possible

MEDITERRANEAN

← Blue ombré tiles lighten up the guest bathrooms

MEDITERRANEAN

# THE ESSENCE OF IBIZA STYLE

Neutral colours, built-in furniture, stone, natural materials, organic shapes – this typical finca ticks all the boxes of the ever-popular Ibiza look.

Instantly recognisable with its natural materials and whitewashed textured walls, the local vernacular is perfectly encapsulated in this 800-square-metre typical finca by Bloom Studio. 'The aim was to create peaceful spaces with individual touches that result in a modern home, but without renouncing traditional architecture,' explain the designers. 'The essential elements of the design were to guarantee continuity throughout the whole property so that every room felt homely and luxurious, and to maximise the communal spaces to allow guests to feel comfortable in the different areas which make up the house.' The studio used a great deal of natural stone throughout the whole project, from the bathrooms to the kitchen and the floor, while the colour palette was kept neutral to create a serene feel. The materials that were chosen reflect the island, while a touch of luxury was added with bright, golden taps throughout all the bathrooms.

'The idea behind the project as a whole was to retain this traditional Ibizan feel by valuing the finca's existing design while also taking modern needs into account,' they continue.

'The finishes and choice of materials give a nod to the island's natural colour palette, and the spaces were planned to make sure the house worked for a family. Without compromising the needs of the kitchen and pantry, details were added to maximise the space, like creating a bar between the kitchen and dining room to combine the two areas, with long lunches and dinners in mind.'

At the same time, the project sought to pay tribute to the stonework in the living room, further fostering that sense of history and the relationship with the island. Another way of underlining the idiosyncrasies of the island was through the furnishings. 'The furniture we chose reflected the materials used in the design; light neutral palettes were considered when choosing sofas and beds, while plush rugs were used to soften larger areas. Every little detail was taken into account when it came to the design of the glass doors, to ensure the style worked with the original architecture.

The idea behind the project as a whole was to retain the traditional Ibizan feel by valuing the finca's existing design while also taking modern needs into account

The aim was to create peaceful spaces with individual touches that result in a modern home, but without renouncing traditional architecture.

We could almost talk about a kind of understated luxury, evident in aspects like the built-in lights, the metal finishes, the restoration of original features, the stonework, the niches and the furniture. Every element was painstakingly thought through to create that sense of tranquillity across the project.'

Dividing the entrances with arches is something very local, just like the built-in furniture. These are elements that the house seems to quietly generate, creating a play and a dialogue with the rest of the pieces. Combining everything with materials like hemp, rattan or wicker and balancing them with a counterpoint of dark accents using side tables, textiles or paintings leads to an interpretation one step beyond Mediterranean style. This house coins its own particular style, one that reflects the elegance of those who live here, and the result is textbook Ibiza.

← The finishes and choice of materials give a nod to the island's natural colour palette, and the spaces were planned to make sure the house worked for a family

MEDITERRANEAN

Every element was painstakingly thought through to create a sense of tranquillity across the house, from the colour palette to the stonework and small niches.

Dividing entrances with arches is a very local design feature. An Eichholtz 'Elan' armchair with brushed brass frame and bouclé upholstery brings a touch of mid-century style ←

Eichholtz's 'Donato' bar stools line the white marble bar that links the kitchen and dining room. The kitchen can be closed off using the folding glazed panels ↓

135

MEDITERRANEAN

←←
The furniture's light neutral palette brings a sense of peace and tranquillity to the space. Plush rugs and curved designs such as Eichholtz's 'Palla' pillows are used to soften larger areas

→
Neutral colours, built-in furniture, stone, natural materials and organic shapes – this bedroom represents the classic Mediterranean style

MEDITERRANEAN

The design brief was to guarantee continuity throughout the whole property so that every room felt homely and luxurious – even the children's room, where a pair of Dart Home rugs bring a sense of fun

MEDITERRANEAN

# OLD MEETS NEW

Remodelled by Bloom Studio, this traditional finca boasts beautifully preserved original features and carefully curated new additions created by local craftspeople.

Founded by architect Kit Maplethorpe, Ibiza and London-based Bloom Studio aims to fuse architecture and interior design to create spaces with timeless appeal. Its interior design team, headed by Sarah Elkabas, fashions unique, highly detailed spaces for each of their clients. One such is Casa G, a 380-square-metre traditional finca home with five en-suite bathrooms. The design studio was tasked with modernising the interior without losing the essence of the original architecture. 'The aim was to enhance the original features but at the same time create a more functional house. The bathrooms, for example, were designed with a view to giving them a contemporary touch. The natural stone vanities contrast with the copper-toned sanitary ware, which creates a balance between old and new throughout the whole space. A traditional kitchen was also retained, but with a more modern worktop and custom-made hardware,' say the designers.

As you pass through the property, you find the most contemporary elements juxtaposed with the oldest original features. At Bloom Studio, the aim is always to preserve the essence of a place rather than create empty, modern white boxes. By listening to the building, and imagining its history and the lives that have passed through it, they can follow a respectful architectural and interior design approach. As well as sandblasting the original beams to celebrate the property's rustic heritage, the designers have remodelled the rooms to make them more functional, and installed an elegant new staircase. Featuring bespoke ironwork by local blacksmith Beltrame and natural stones tiles from Almería, it allows light to flow through the house, and encourages communication across different rooms and levels.

'We have added unique details across the property, like the bespoke stone desks and counters, and have carefully chosen materials which, although they might be modern, don't stand out within the scheme,' they explain. 'The general design was relaxed luxury, and the idea is that you'll be pleasantly surprised as you walk through the interior.' And they have certainly achieved just that.

The white staircase is finished with a simple forged black metal railing by local blacksmith Beltrame, allowing light to flow and encouraging communication across different levels

It is a traditional Ibizan finca with one large living space and a succession of rooms that open onto the main communal area.

→ In the living area is a built-in curved sofa, so typical of the Ibizan style; a sweeping semi-circle, promoting eye contact at all times and perfect for social gatherings. The 'Chapeau' pendant light, accessories and decorative items add an ethnic feel

The built-in curved sofa, so typical of the Ibizan style, creates a sweeping semi-circle, promoting eye contact at all times and perfectly suited to social gatherings, while there is a clear Eastern influence, which comes through in the little side tables and decorative items.

The exposed wooden ceiling is a delightful feature that envelops the upper floor, and thanks to a series of subtle, hidden lighting, it is capable of turning a bedroom or bathroom into a cosy, welcoming refuge. Small niches housing decorative items and an intense dialogue with the outside space round off a project that truly defines the Bloom Studio style.

MEDITERRANEAN

→ The are no doors or dividing walls between the master bedroom and bathroom, so the free-standing bathtub becomes one of the decorative features of the room

MEDITERRANEAN

← The traditional finca's exterior is pure Ibiza, with dark-green fronds contrasting with the bright white facade

145

COSMOPOLITAN
ECLECTIC
MEDITERRANEAN
**MID-CENTURY**
**INTERIORS**
COLOURFUL
SOBER

# 04

MID-CENTURY

# FROM MIAMI TO IBIZA

Interior designer Caroline Legrand found this little piece of paradise and made it her own, turning away from the rustic white that is so typical of the island. Her secret? A perfect mix of 1970s vintage and the exuberance of Palm Springs.

Interior designer Caroline Legrand managed to fulfil a wish and make the stars align in this villa set on an 80,000-square-metre plot. 'The main house was built in 1995 and consists of two floors. As soon as I saw it, I fell in love, and my dream was to transform this beautiful property into a jewel, but in a style that wasn't contemporary white or farmhouse rustic. I wanted to transcend my favourite era of 1970s chic on the White Isle,' explains Legrand. 'When I bought the house, I was working on three other projects and sourcing furniture – cool mid-century and 1970s pieces – in Miami and Palm Beach. I bought 95 per cent of the furniture, lamps and artwork in Miami and shipped it all to Ibiza in a container. My biggest joy was seeing all the pieces chosen in Miami find a place in the house, one by one, so perfectly. And in my own house! It remains one of my greatest interior design achievements.'

Caroline's vision for her holiday home was clear from the outset. 'I wanted to keep the interior cool, in both senses of the word, while keeping an easy connection with the outdoors. Being a summer house, it had to be light and airy, but avoiding that all-white, bohemian look which is so popular on the island.' So Caroline did it her way, using a palette of caramel, tan, nutmeg, beige, cream, rust, tobacco and white throughout the house. Splashes of cobalt blue were added to tie in with the original tiles in the swimming pool: white-and-cobalt striped cushions on the pool loungers, and antique cobalt ceramic vases in the main house. Natural materials and textures, as well as organic fabrics, were also key elements. Shaggy rugs, organic wool curtains and cork wallpaper in the cabana give warmth and a certain retro whimsy.

The main house consists of 220 square metres spread over two floors, with living room, open-plan kitchen, bathroom and guest bedroom with en-suite bathroom on the ground floor and a first floor with two bedrooms with en-suite bathrooms, another bedroom and a large outdoor terrace. The first project was to convert an unwanted garage into a comfortable cabana for guests and add a gym at the rear. 'I incorporated large glass windows to create sweeping views of

Caroline Legrand wanted to create a 1970s feel – her favourite era – and was delighted when, one by one, all the pieces she had bought in Miami found their perfect place in the house

149

'I wanted to keep the interior cool, in every sense of the word, and keep an easy connection with the outdoors.'

the garden, to recreate a Palm Springs feel,' Caroline says. The inspiration for the outdoor bedroom for her two teenage sons at the time (now grown up), came from a page in US *Vogue*. Since entertaining is an important part of life in Ibiza, Caroline concentrated on designing a chill-out zone in the garden, with a large wooden dining table and outdoor kitchen with barbeque. A sunken seating area is centred around a spectacular pine tree, with a fabulous centre-piece table made of Yosemite wood.

Caroline's expert eye has resulted in a practical yet stylish holiday house, beautifully designed to balance glamour and earthiness. Her aesthetic is based on a simple premise: 'I want to live with things that bring me joy every time I look at them.'

The aim throughout was to keep the interior cool, in every sense of the word, whilst creating an easy connection with the outdoors; the living room is a perfect example of this

→ The original garden was already spectacular, so all that was needed was a stunning pool to make the most of the wonderful climate

MID-CENTURY

A chill-out zone was created in the garden, with a large wooden dining table and outdoor kitchen with barbeque

MID-CENTURY

# URBAN OASIS

Interior designer Caroline Legrand calls this project Casa Sydney, as this new-build house in Cala Llonga emanates the bold, urban elegance of Australia's most celebrated city.

Casa Sydney is unusual – a modern, four-storey townhouse, with a rooftop pool and terrace – and is not at all how you would imagine a house in Ibiza. Its eclectic mix of furniture and contemporary elements somehow come together to create a sophisticated style, not often seen on an island like Ibiza. The challenging brief to the designer was to conjure up a very cool metropolitan city, while at the same time keeping a casual and sporty feel, in a place that invites you to live a more bohemian lifestyle. 'What I like most about this project is that it took me completely by surprise,' explains Legrand. 'I was excited when my client asked me to come on board as this is very different from anything I had done before. I started to put the design ideas together while the house was still a building site but the base materials for this new design canvas were quite chic and simple, with a palette with which I could work easily.'

Spread over 400 square metres, the house is 'set in a very complicated site, as the land has a very steep slope with a 15-metre gradient,' as its owner Adrian explains. 'This has been utilised to create the staggered levels of the house, and the pool is located on the roof, with panoramic views of the sea and mountains.' On the ground floor there is a garage, gym, sauna and playroom. The main living and dining spaces are on the first floor, along with the kitchen, a wine cellar, cool room and a guest bathroom. There is also a large terrace with views of the trees and the sea. The second floor has three bedrooms and a small patio and garden. Once again, this floor has large terraces overlooking the scenery. The third floor is the master bedroom (accessible by a lift as well as the stairs) with an outdoor bathing area and direct access to the roof terrace. The rooftop pool is very cool with plush beds all along the poolside and incredible views. 'I used a lot of rattan furniture on the terrace and added palm trees to make it even greener,' explains the designer.

In terms of textures and materials, the floors are light-grey stone, which is actually warmer than concrete. And although white is predominant in the house, the designer used a richer colour palette with elements seldom

Set on a slope, the plot was tricky to develop yet still manages to boast a lavish pool surrounded by an orchard

Being located on a slope meant it was possible to take advantage of the 15-metre gradient to create the entire house using staggered levels.

seen in a beach house, like textured wallpaper. 'People seem to be afraid of using wallpaper in Ibiza, but like anything, it can be a winning element if you know how to use it.'

If there is a space Legrand is particularly proud of, it is without a doubt the living room. 'The house has so many rooms and is spacious, but the living room isn't big and, with the kitchen having quite a presence with its blue/grey slate effect and gold stools, I felt that the sitting room had to be as organic as possible and have a shape and an identity of its own. I knew from the beginning that with everything being square in the house, a circular sofa would add personality, and I found the perfect one by Giacomo Passera.' A Harvey Probber cabinet, a Jonathan Adler coffee table and a huge lamp were all the extras that were needed. Who says urban style can't work in a beach house? Here we have proof that it can.

→ The gold dining table, ceiling lights and bar stool are balanced by a pure white circular Giacomo Passera sofa, bringing personality and comfort to the living room

MID-CENTURY

'People seem to be afraid of using wallpaper in Ibiza, but like anything it can a winning element if you know how to use it.'

An original ethnic style lamp by Pols Potten takes centre stage in the bedroom ←

Style is in the details, and this niche is certainly not lacking either ↓

159

MID-CENTURY

# MOORISH MEETS DISCO

Two conflicting decorative concepts and yet an amazing final result. Rebekka Eliza's photographs perfectly capture Kourosh Ghadishah and Jasmien Hamed's peculiar style.

As eclectic as it is functional, this 200-year-old villa retains plenty of original features, while at the same time integrating contemporary elements brilliantly. Hacienda Nomad – alias Kourosh Ghadishah and Jasmien Hamed – decided the best thing to do was preserve the style, with its clear Moorish influence, and adapted to the house rather than the other way around.

The 350-square-metre house is located on a 3,000-square-metre plot on the outskirts of Santa Eulalia del Río, and is surrounded by farmland – ' in fact, it is one of the very first farmhouses to be built along this stretch of the old road to Santa Eulalia,' say the designers. The finca comprises three bedrooms in the main house, and two in the casita, a fabulous walled patio with a Moorish fountain facing the living room, swimming pool, open-air shower and an entire leisure area just outside the kitchen. Later additions include a spacious living room, the circular entrance hall and a master bedroom.

'The additions were made in a Moorish/Andalucian style, clearly evident in the windows, arches and the patio with its central fountain. When we moved into the house, in July 2021, we renovated the kitchen and one of the upstairs bedrooms.' When it came to the structure of the house, 'the bones of it were already there, and were incredible, so all we had to do was bring it up to date, modernise certain areas and make them more functional.' The pair took great pleasure in remodelling and updating the kitchen, for example, using microcement for worktops and cupboards. The arches and shelves are original, as are the hand-printed tiles. The duo was very clear that there were certain pieces they absolutely had to have. 'The large sheepskin sofa: it's a great sofa for parties and for watching movies in winter. And the disco ball, of course! Every home needs a disco ball! We ended up hanging ours in the old well outside, beside the outdoor shower.'

Ultimately, every house is a reflection of those who live in it, and in this case the inspiration came from the owners' travels and from their collection sourced from art and antiques

Built 200 years ago, the finca clearly had an Arabic influence that Hacienda Nomad took great pains to preserve, bringing it up to date but maintaining its unique style

**The villa is 200 years old and is thought to be one of the first Ibizan farmhouses to be built along this stretch of the old road to Santa Eulalia.**

fairs. 'We didn't really follow any interior trends per se, but rather designed each room so it had unique pieces that somehow work together,' say the designers. 'We found amazing second-hand furniture from private vendors, markets and auctions and gave them a new lease of life, like the yellow Milo Baughman swivel chairs. We bought or designed some of the furniture ourselves in places like Marrakech and Bali. One example is the Frank Gehry–inspired swivel chairs, made in bamboo instead of cardboard. Our favourite artworks are the bird painting by Jon Ching, the modern painting by artist Julie Harris and the Calder-esque mobile. The wooden glass cabinet came from Casa Polanski, the Ibizan home of Roman Polanski. It was one of the pieces he left behind when he sold the house to our friend David Leppan. The Platner dining chairs in the circular living room with all the plants (the entrance hall) are from a flea market in Palm Springs. Some of the decorative items like the clay pots on the shelves come from Morocco.' A very groovy mix, we say.

→ The Moorish-style windows form an exotic backdrop to an eclectic collection including a pair of chairs from Bali

MID-CENTURY

'We didn't really follow any interior trends, but rather designed each room so it had unique pieces that somehow work together.'

Abstract Moroccan pottery line the shelves in the living room, a welcoming space that also features a pair of yellow swivel Milo Baughman armchairs

The dining area features Warren Platner chairs and a custom-made chandelier from Bali

The kitchen was renovated using microcement for worktops and cupboard units

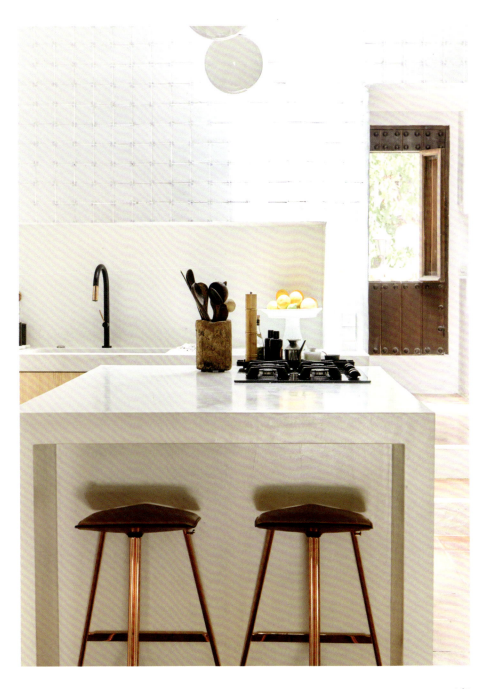

MID-CENTURY

→ A pair of rattan folding chairs await by the swimming pool. Every house is a reflection of those who live in it, and in this case the inspiration came from the owners' travels, visits to art and antiques fairs, and collection of unique pieces

MID-CENTURY

A disco ball hangs above the old well, just next to the outdoor shower

COSMOPOLITAN
ECLECTIC
MEDITERRANEAN
MID-CENTURY
**COLOURFUL
INTERIORS**
SOBER

05

COLOURFUL

# THE WORK OF A LIFETIME

Architect and interior designer Luis Galliussi stumbled upon this derelict farmhouse over 20 years ago. He has been making it his own ever since, turning Can Kaki into a peaceful sanctuary.

It all started at a friend's dinner party back in 1999, when Luis Galliussi, originally from Argentina, sat next to a wonderful woman who insisted on showing him the island and its houses, to see if there was anything he'd like to buy. 'The idea had never occurred to me; I had always preferred to have somewhere within easy reach by land, and have a place two hours from Madrid at most,' he explains. 'I agreed to have a look around the island but nothing called out to me, and besides, it all seemed like a lot of money. The tour was coming to an end and this poor woman told me, not sounding very optimistic, to go and have a look at some place where there was a very small, abandoned ruin. I did, and I loved it; I could feel the soul of the place immediately. And that was how I decided.'

The house is named after Luis's beloved dog Kaki. 'I found my adored Kaki, who is no longer with me, at the Sant Jordi market – a native Ibizan through and through,' says the designer. 'Can Kaki is my paradise, my refuge. I've worked on the garden myself and the idea was to preserve what was already there: almond, carob, olive and orange trees. I simply restored what was already planted in the terraces and gradually added native species and some fruit trees like apricots, figs, medlars and vines, taking care to avoid anything that needs lots of water. Ibiza is an island without water. The only thing I allowed myself was rose bushes, a flower I love to have at home; old roses.'

The house itself is in S'Estanyol, a tranquil bay with a sandy beach, and covers around 250 square metres, with a hectare of land. Luis has renovated it three times already: 'During the first remodelling, just after I bought it, I respected the spirit of what was already here, and took it from there. That sense of respect was so strong that I left all the little doorways and windows exactly where they had been in the original farmhouse; I just wanted to enhance them to make it habitable, without destroying the soul of the place. The layout remained the same: the kitchen, a small living room, my bedroom and a bathroom, as well as a separate small guest house, also with a bathroom. In the second intervention, in 2007, I added what is now the living

Luis Galliussi has spent the past 20 years making Can Kaki into a sanctuary to enjoy alone and with friends. Entering the house, you feel you are entering a place as personal as it is loved, where every detail speaks of its owner

173

'The sense of respect was so strong that I left all the little doorways and windows exactly where they had been; I just wanted to enhance them, without destroying the soul of the place.'

room, aiming for comfort and generosity when it came to the proportions, materials and natural light, without compromising that delicate atmosphere by making sure not to stifle its origins or lose sight of the fact that this is Ibiza. And then in 2009 I added two more bedrooms, two bathrooms and the swimming pool.'

Full of natural light, the south-facing house has very thick walls of up to 60 centimetres, covered in traditional whitewash paint to allow the walls to breathe, while pergolas with sticks or reeds to create patches of dappled shade. 'The decor is very Galliussi, nothing premeditated, incorporating pieces I already owned and some that I find as I go along,' says the designer. 'I'm obsessed with fabrics. There are things from every corner of the world, some very important, others far less so. Egypt, Argentina, the US, France, Portugal, Uruguay, Morocco, Spain, Mexico. Every time I travel, I bring something back for my homes, and they also travel between them; I move things from one house to another. The floor is cement tiles, and I chose large ones, 50 by 50 centimetres I kept the typical stone of the Balearic Islands that can be seen in the white and earthy tones of the walls. If I'm asked about my inspiration, it would be observing the origins of rural and Nubian architecture; an introverted, austere and totally sustainable notion of architecture.'

→ The architecture and layout is all very simple: south-facing and full of natural light throughout, very thick walls of up to 60 centimetres and traditional whitewash paint

COLOURFUL

⬅⬅ All the little doorways and windows were left exactly where they had been in the original farmhouse

⬅ The decor is very casual, and everywhere you look you see pieces that tell a story of a previous life or were brought back from distant travels

➡ The typical Balearic Islands stone was maintained, seen in the walls. Some were whitewashed and others left in their original state

COLOURFUL

← The architecture is introverted, austere and totally sustainable

COLOURFUL

'The decor is very Galliussi, nothing premeditated, incorporating pieces I already owned and some that I find as I go along. I'm obsessed with fabrics. There are things from every corner of the world.'

→ A simple wooden table and benches – the perfect place to enjoy afternoons and evenings on the island

↓ The simple swimming pool overlooks a lush wooded hillside

COLOURFUL

→

Galliussi kept his bedroom deliberately small to leave more space for the other rooms. The simple bed, with tables, plants and a typical small window, define the space

182

COLOURFUL

←

In the courtyard garden, the idea was to preserve what was already there – almond, carob, olive and orange trees, adding native species and some fruit trees such as apricots, figs, medlars and vines – taking care to avoid anything that needs lots of water

COLOURFUL

# SEVENTIES CHIC

This Dutch family's home and studio riffs on Ibiza's 1970s Adlib fashion style with an eye-catching blend of rustic elements and pops of bright colours.

Named after the Latin expression *ad libitum*, meaning 'with freedom', Ibiza's Adlib fashion style appeared in the 1970s, merging traditional local elements such as straw hats, espadrilles and shawls with hippie, flower-power influences. Spearheaded by expat Smila Mihailovitch and locals such as José Colomar, Adlib fashion took the world by storm with its 'wear what you want, but do it with style' motto, and focus on rustic, handcrafted materials and flowing light fabrics.

And something of that freedom is definitely present in the decor of Can Curralasos, a 460-square-metre, newly built villa. Comprising a living room and lounge, kitchen/diner, TV room and three bedrooms, as well as a 70-square-metre two bedroom guesthouse, it is owned by a Dutch family who were originally looking for a holiday home, but ended up falling in love with the house so much that they relocated to live there all year round. To give a little 'soul' to this perfect building – using traditional elements like plastered walls, beamed ceilings, built-in wardrobes and skylights – the owners entrusted Rolf Blakstad, head of Blakstad Design Consultants, with the overall design. But the family itself took care of the interior, since owner Hetty is a children's fashion designer and therefore well placed to unleash her boundless creativity in this new space of hers.

With its pristine whiteness and high ceilings so typical of Ibizan buildings as a background, the villa is filled with a perfect compendium of carefully selected furniture, art and design pieces, and a rainbow of colour, splashing each and every corner of the house with joy. Conceived as a continuous series of rooms without doors and an endless sense of space, it has found warmth through the bold creative additions of its owners.

A certain Arabic inspiration is apparent in the furniture and textiles, as well as the structural details and flooring, achieving a perfect mix of periods and styles. From start to finish, the project has been driven by deep respect for its roots. To channel a hippie vibe, the original wooden windows and partitions have been retained, while the tapestries and rugs in different

Conceived as a continuous series of rooms without doors, the house boasts an endless sense of space and is filled with unexpected bursts of colour, such as this yellow Panton chair

With its pristine whiteness and high ceilings so typical of Ibizan buildings as a backdrop, the house is filled with a perfect compendium of carefully selected furniture, design pieces and a rainbow of colour.

textures and colours provide a balanced counterpoint to the classic and contemporary design pieces,.

Made for slow living, Can Curralasos boasts wonderful views of the countryside, as well as a well-manicured garden with swimming pool, allowing you to live outside when the weather permits, which is more often than not. A palm tree here, an Ingo Maurer lamp there, a Tom Dixon stool... Nothing has been left to chance, and yet it manages to convey that sense of serendipity that defines the essence of the Balearic Islands.

→ A whitewashed patio leads to the swimming pool area

COLOURFUL

A certain Arabic inspiration is apparent in the furniture and textiles as well as the structural details and flooring, achieving a perfect mix of periods and styles.

The pristine white walls are a blank canvas for splashes of colour that come through in the furniture and artwork, such as the yellow chair by Kartel and the vintage pink sofa

In the living room, the white walls and sofa by Living Divani create a stark contrast with the colourful cushions, stool and the Amini rug

Built-in display shelves house the owner's treasured items

COLOURFUL

→ Textiles take centre stage in rooms like this bedroom, against soft, simple details like a hanging plant and the white-painted beams

COLOURFUL

← The main bedroom features a stunning original ceiling, a 'Manila' chair by Val Padilla for Conran, and more colourful fabrics

COLOURFUL

# THE BEAT GOES ON

The home of journalist Laura Martínez and businessman Diego Calvo pays tribute to the wild hedonism of Italy's Dolce Vita era and, above all, the Palm Springs home of Sonny & Cher.

Sometimes simply taking your dog for a longer walk can lead to an unexpected find – perhaps a glimpse of an old house with a balcony. And that chance encounter can then turn into a momentous project, as the journalist Laura Martínez and businessman Diego Calvo, co-founder of the Concept Hotel Group, found out. 'The truth is, it was the house that found us and not the other way around,' they say. 'It was a stroke of luck as we were out walking with our dachshund Romeo. We lived about ten minutes down the road but never used to go so high on our walks. That day Romeo led us to an old house with a well-kept appearance, painted and with a lattice balcony, which looked to have a lot of land on different levels. We couldn't see much more over the fence, but destiny ensured it was ours soon after. We called it Villa Carmelita, after Sonny & Cher's house on a hill in Palm Springs, which was renowned for its glamourous parties in the 1970s.'

The building dates back to 1936 and is located in the heart of Sant Josep, Sa Carroca – a luxurious rural spot in Ibiza with panoramic views that span from Las Salinas to Cap des Falcó, via the island of Formentera, which can be seen perfectly outlined on clear days. As the terrain is terraced, the layout was planned across several areas: 'The covered porch near the swimming pool area, which we call Il Giardinetto, was a dry field full of orange trees, so we chose to cover it with gravel and add a tiled table from the Costa del Sol for lunches and dinners, with the "Maremoto" parasol by Lobster's Day, a solar-powered water fountain for making wishes and a pair of columns with Italian Baroque-style vases' explain the owners. 'We also planted a small lemon tree and placed the wonderful "Cubanito" chairs and table by iSiMAR, with a reclining sun lounger from The Maisie to doze off in with a book at sunset.' As the house is white, it lent itself to a play of colour, and Laura and Diego wanted to evoke a Palm Springs style, settling on shades of lime green and salmon pink, with splashes of bright yellow.

'We were clear that the house's strong point was the outside space, and in Ibiza it's where you spend most time, so we poured all our love into it. Villa Carmelita is a

← Villa Carmelita is a reflection of the creative universe of Diego Calvo, co-founder of the Concept Hotel Group, and journalist Laura Martínez's passion for everything related to the 1960s and 1970s

**The building dates back to 1936 and is located in the heart of Sant Josep, Sa Carroca – a luxurious rural spot in Ibiza with panoramic views.**

→ Dating back to 1936, the villa is located in the heart of Sant Josep, Sa Carroca – a luxurious rural spot with privileged views that span from Las Salinas to Cap des Falcó, via the island of Formentera

reflection of Diego's creative universe and my passion for everything related to the 1960s and 1970s,' Laura says. 'As a journalist I always tend to look back, and I'm inspired by everything that happened in those times when there was so much cultural effervescence in every part of life, and where they dressed, lived, danced and enjoyed themselves so damn well. It's a mix of our two worlds, our shared philosophy of joie de vivre and the hedonism of *la dolce vita* that we used to accentuate the character of the house. Ultimately, if you put Diego and Laura together, what you get in aesthetic terms is Villa Carmelita.' A home, without a doubt, designed to be party central.

COLOURFUL

←

Once a dry field full of orange trees, the pool area now features checkerboard tiles matching the vintage martini bar, as well as 'Maremoto' parasols by Lobster's Day

→

The project embraced anything with a 1970s vibe, such as this retro Italian dining set, conjuring up the atmosphere of Sonny & Cher's Palm Springs home and the glamourous parties they hosted

COLOURFUL

In the dining area, fun lime-green chairs from Lobster's Day define the space, while a framed photograph by Slim Aarons emphasises the 1970s vibe

COLOURFUL

As the house is white, it lent itself to a play of colour, and Laura and Diego settled on shades of lime green and salmon pink, with splashes of bright yellow.

A pink 'wiggle' mirror by ilmiodesign and a roaring porcelain panther by El Recibidor colour the hallway ←

In case their style was ever in question, this vintage record player and vinyl collection with a Julio Iglesias LP sleeve on top leaves no room for doubt ↓

COLOURFUL

# A SLICE OF BRAZILIAN MID-CENTURY STYLE

The Brazilian heritage of one of the owners is celebrated with understated modernist armchairs and vibrant colours. An effortlessly elegant space designed by Natalia Miyar.

Located in Sant Agustí des Vedrà, this villa is a new-build property spread over 1,000 square metres, which fuses the magic of Ibiza with elements inspired by Rio de Janeiro, one of the owners' hometowns. 'This Brazilian heritage is celebrated in muted mid-century armchairs that complement the vibrant colours and add an air of effortless chic to the mix,' explains the London-based designer Natalia Miyar. 'Downstairs, bold silk wallcoverings sit alongside playful patterning and motifs. This modernist private holiday home has been modelled and crafted to reflect and respect the beauty of the nature surrounding it. Rich rust, greens and blues so intrinsic to the island's palette are radiant within the fresh white walls.'

The owners insisted on several essentials that had to be included in the project, such as a large bookcase and some marble tables that belonged to the family. The Brazilian-style armchairs mentioned above not only set the tone for the personality of the project but somehow also actually became the driving force behind the rest of the furniture and decoration. 'And in the background, as if floating over every space, the huge artworks by Olafur Eliasson,' says Miyar. 'They were without doubt the inspiration for the colour combination.' Each room is defined by a different paint colour, with printed fabrics and wallpaper, following the same pattern that Eliasson uses in his pieces.

When Miyar is asked about the materials used to bring the project together, she talks of wood, 'lots of wood'; coloured tiles used in the kitchen to add yet more personality; colourful upholstery and patterns inspired by works of art; her own Ambia fabric wallcovering in bespoke colour combinations; and even some vintage stone and ceramic pieces thrown into the mix.

Another important element was the light. The house boasts a great deal of natural light, which has been maximised at every opportunity. Skylights have been installed, while large glass doors lead out onto the garden from every room. A

*A huge, cosmic artwork by Olafur Eliasson hangs in the living room*

Bold silk wall coverings are combined with stylish and fun patterns and motifs, echoing the mid-century vibe.

→ A mix of materials were used to give the project depth, like the coloured tiles that add personality in the kitchen. On the wall is an artwork by Mary Stephenson

bespoke dining room chandelier and the Stephen Antonson table lamp deserve their own special mention.

The large windows merge inside with outside in a discreet yet decisive way. The landscape surrounding the villa is green and lush, so that from the inside the house could pass as a beautiful woodland cabin. Yet it remains Ibiza through and through, with its sea and its salt, its breeze and its colours, and allowing all that to flow through the finca was imperative. The straight, simple lines, the pops of colour that seem to introduce elements of the sea and sand, and organic shapes in the furniture and decoration create that sought-after tranquillity which encourages reflection and observation. It conjures a sense of being surrounded by elements from another country, another era, but which nevertheless marry perfectly with the design that Miyar envisaged and carried through from start to finish.

COLOURFUL

The huge Olafur Eliasson artworks provided the inspiration for the colour palette.

Inspired by Brazilian modernist architecture, the villa features a sleek covered patio area and is surrounded by a large garden

The large windows merge inside with outside in a discreet yet decisive way

Each room is defined by a different paint colour, with printed fabrics and wallpaper. In the living room the wallpaper 'Ambia' by Natalia Miyar adds a fun touch

COLOURFUL

211

↑
This modernist private holiday home has been modelled and designed to reflect and respect the beauty of the nature surrounding it

COLOURFUL

← Organic shapes in the furniture and decoration create the sought-after tranquillity which encourages reflection and observation

COSMOPOLITAN
ECLECTIC
MEDITERRANEAN
MID-CENTURY
COLOURFUL
**SOBER
INTERIORS**

06

SOBER

# BLENDING INTO THE LANDSCAPE

Framework Studio is the name behind this exclusive villa, designed to be totally absorbed by the landscape and with a traditional yet contemporary design.

Set in the middle of a plot of over 8 hectares, with a unique, secluded mountainside location with high elevation and sea views, this 480-square-metre family home seems to disappear into the landscape. It is as though it is trying to go unnoticed, allowing nature and the environment to envelop everything. This, at least, was the premise on which architecture and design firm Framework Studio based its design. The owners' brief contained another challenge: to build using traditional design and architecture, but with a subtle blend of contemporary elements.

'We love quality, craftmanship and relationships. We always design the architecture of a building according to its geographical location,' says Thomas Geerlings, the Dutch founder of Framework Studio, whose HQ is in Amsterdam, with branches in Paris and Ibiza.

Can Brut's gardens are filled with lush flowers, with bees and small birds flying all around. Exterior corridors lead visitors along the slopes of the mountain to one of the villa's entrances. The essence of the island can be felt in the facades, clad in local stone, which emulate the dry-stone walls that line the roads in Ibiza. As you enter, the huge doors flood the hallway with light and the space opens up into the kitchen area, leading the eye to the lower levels via a spiral staircase that connects the house. The kitchen is a unique space, made to measure by the studio itself, developed with an elegant mix of Roman travertine, natural oak and gunmetal. The sense of space in the villa is enhanced by the curved ceilings that reference traditional building methods, but also by hidden skylights throughout that direct daylight into its heart. When the sun goes down, cylindrical spotlights by lighting specialists PSLab provide just the right accent, inside and out. The rooms all enjoy views overlooking the garden and are full of interesting design pieces that have been collected over the years.

The kitchen and living rooms are situated near the pool and outdoor dining area, where the family spend most of their time. This is arguably one of the most stunning spaces.

The pool at Can Brut is lined with a green marble called Lapponia, while the terrace and stairs were made of Roman Travertine

217

**The essence of the island can be felt in the facades, clad in local stone, which emulate the dry-stone walls that line the roads in Ibiza.**

→ The bespoke kitchen is an elegant mix of Roman travertine, natural oak and gunmetal, with all of the clutter hidden from sight

Surrounded by limestone, the pool is lined with a wonderful green marble called Lapponia. The staircases outside were made with Roman Travertine, which was also used in the interior. The scene is crowned with superb views of the wooded landscape, and the Mediterranean Sea on the horizon. This environment, together with the centuries-old junipers, creates that magical feeling that arises when you are completely isolated and off the beaten track.

Walking around the villa, the landscape is ever-present, due to the changes in level in the property, as well as its finishes, materials and the colour palette used, in keeping with the lines used throughout the project. The space feels playful and open, while the contour curves give the visitor a sense of privacy within the open-plan layouts.

SOBER

← The sense of space in the villa is enhanced by the curved ceilings that reference traditional building methods, but also by hidden skylights throughout that direct daylight into its heart

→ The owners were keen for the studio to develop a scheme that used traditional design and architecture, but with a subtle blend of contemporary elements such as the Sculptural Sectional sofa group by Wiener Wersträtten from 1970

SOBER

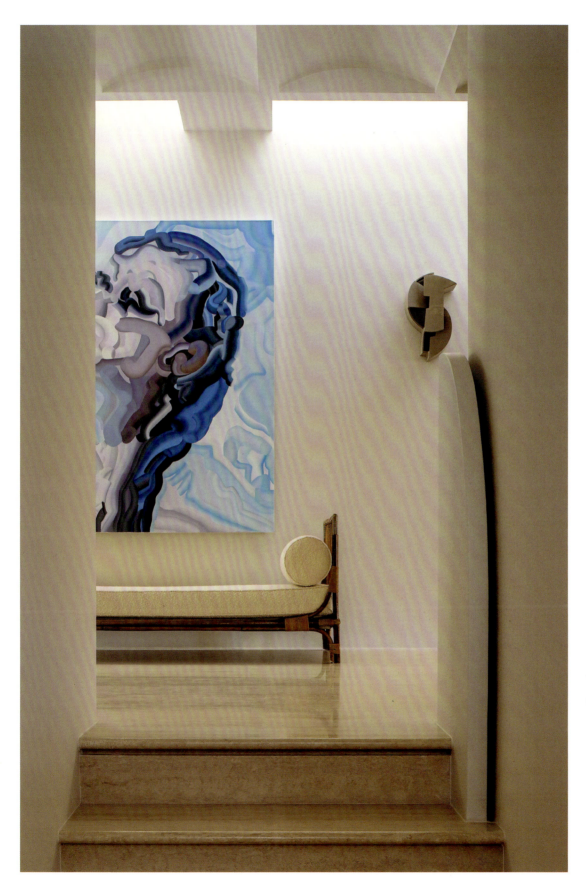

← The artwork by Ding Li adds a splash of colour to the hallway

SOBER

Surrounded by limestone and lined with a green marble called Lapponia, the swimming pool makes a huge visual impact.

Natural fabrics like the linen curtains, the raw wood of the table by José Zanine Caldas and artisan ceramics are carefully combined to emphasise local elements, but with a distinctly elegant touch

The essence of the island can be felt in the facades, clad in local stone, which emulate the dry-stone walls that line the roads in Ibiza. This environment, together with the centuries-old junipers, creates that magical feeling that arises when you are completely isolated and off the beaten track

225

SOBER

←

When the sun goes down, cylindrical spotlights by lighting specialists PSLab provide the perfect accent, inside and out, further enhancing the sense of space and elegance of the communal areas. The artwork on the wall by Nerone Patuzzi adds an extra element of warmth to the space

→

The rooms all enjoy views over the garden and are full of interesting design pieces that have been collected over the years

228

SOBER

← The project's key elements of craftsmanship, organic lines and respect for traditions are sustained even in the children's bedroom

229

SOBER

# LOOKING BACK, LOOKING EAST

An eclectic mix of influences, this family retreat is inspired among other things by Japan's wabi-sabi culture and medieval ornamentation. The resulting home perfectly combines antiques, handcrafted artisan techniques, restored pieces and industrial elements.

A far cry from the archetypal summer house on the island of light and partying, Can Pep offers shade and tranquillity, taking inspiration from wabi-sabi, a Japanese aesthetic term based on the beauty of imperfection. The main property retains a typical Mediterranean style – thick walls, Sabina wood ceiling beams and tiny windows that barely let in any sunlight – while the annex, featured here, has been completely renovated into a five-bedroom home by Ibiza's El Contempo studio.

A barn which would have originally been used as a food store and tool shed, 'the building consists of a large single-storey space with concrete walls and two large openings,' the designers Gilles Tavernier and Ariadna Puigdomenech explain. 'We wanted to maintain the scenographic atmosphere of the old part, to ensure coherence and connection between the two zones, although we wanted to soften the contrast, making it a relaxed and pleasant family retreat. We took advantage of the high ceilings and the two large existing openings, to create one vast expanse, with lots of natural light, thus creating a real sense of space. We kept the existing industrial elements, like the two steel ceiling beams, and unified them by toning down the space with a dark wall texture as well as a stainless-steel kitchen island and a polished concrete worktop. The kitchen and living room are where the family spends most time when they are here. Based on this, we decided to use a long island as the centrepiece of the room, which creates interaction. The island is also the only piece that divides the whole space into two zones: the kitchen area and the living area.'

Almost immediately you feel the warmth that radiates from the colour palette. The secret was to use the same very dim, homogenous tone throughout the space, looking to generate tranquillity and serenity. The colour scheme and choice of materials is neutral and continuous throughout the house. The owners live in London and lead a very busy life, so this holiday home in Ibiza had to be a refuge where they could escape the bustle of the city and recharge their batteries in a relaxed atmosphere, free from distractions.

*The owners live in London and lead a very busy life, so this holiday home in Ibiza had to be a relaxing sanctuary, free from distractions. They certainly fulfilled the brief*

231

**The project is a combination of the influence of Japanese minimalism, medieval ornamentation and 20th-century materials.**

'The story behind the fireplace is wonderful. There had been much talk of wanting to reclaim some hundred-year-old Ibizan stone from the mountain on which the house sits,' explain the designers. 'We thought it was a great idea, and in the end we managed to use the stones as a base for the fireplace, although they first had to be cleaned and restored by local professionals. This became one of our favourite features. For us, materials must have soul.'

The decor also looks to the past for inspiration: 'We were inspired by both the dark corners and the warmth of lighting in ancient castles; every detail is inspired by the furniture of past centuries,' says the El Contempo team. 'We also brought in industrial elements, to give a gentle contrast and make a play on the era of Le Corbusier and Jean Prouvé. By doing away with decorative items, the result is a soft, peaceful, open space, like a Japanese interior. So it could be described as a combination of the influence of Japanese minimalism, medieval ornamentation and 20th-century materials.'

← The fireplace was made using hundred-year-old reclaimed Ibizan stone from the mountain the house is built on. The stones were cleaned and restored by local professionals and used as a base

→ The design studio were inspired by shade, and the warm lighting of ancient castles; every detail is inspired by the furniture of past centuries. They also brought in industrial elements, such as this triple pendant light by Lambert & Fils

SOBER

←

The colour scheme and choice of materials are neutral and continuous throughout the house, with warm, gentle hues – even in the kitchen. Here, the shape of the extractor fan mirrors that of the central fireplace

SOBER

# EARTHY DELIGHTS

Turning the interior into a cool place in which to retreat from the island's searing temperatures is what Hollie Bowden set out to do in this holiday home. Materials such as plaster and concrete and the use of a natural palette were key to her success.

Earthy hues and greys, occasionally black, a splash of blue... The colour palette used in this 350-square-metre finca might not seem like the most typical for Ibiza, an island that constantly bubbles away at boiling point, in an explosion of light, intensity and bright colours. But escaping and taking refuge from all of this is precisely what the owner of this house wanted to do, and designer Hollie Bowden, with her unique talent, was the answer to his prayers.

The truth is, the building itself made things easy. The house is one of those traditional farmhouses that lie scattered across the island, over a hundred years old and with a perfect layout. An open-plan space leads out to the terrace, and at the back of the house a swimming pool boasts views out to sea. It is designed for entertaining, with all of the bedrooms found at the end of corridors and passages, offering a cosy haven away from the party.

When undertaking the renovation, Bowden admits they were not particularly careful to preserve original elements and that they made 'somewhat radical modern interventions, but with natural materials that softened the sharp edges and sat comfortably within a rather traditional framework. It was a matter of leaving space for simplicity, but allowing the nature of the materials to permeate the environment.' The brief was to create a bohemian Ibizan holiday home: serene, unpretentious simplicity with luxurious comfort, a romantic, magical touch, with a great deal of warmth.

All the materials were therefore chosen specifically for their character and the way they help to enhance what was already there, reflecting their surroundings. Plaster and wood take centre stage, together with the concrete floor that is 'so cool and pleasant in hot weather'. Natural carved stone was sourced for the sinks. 'Hemp and natural linens reflect a relaxed comfort. We chose hand-woven fabrics for the upholstered furniture, as well as vintage tapestries and textiles for the walls,' says Bowden. The idea was to keep everything in harmony with the environment by using natural materials, giving the project an organic quality.

The brief was above all to create a bohemian Ibizan holiday home – serene, unpretentious simplicity with luxurious comfort, a romantic, magical touch, and a great deal of warmth. In the bedroom this is obtained by adding the embroideries made by Alexis Gautier

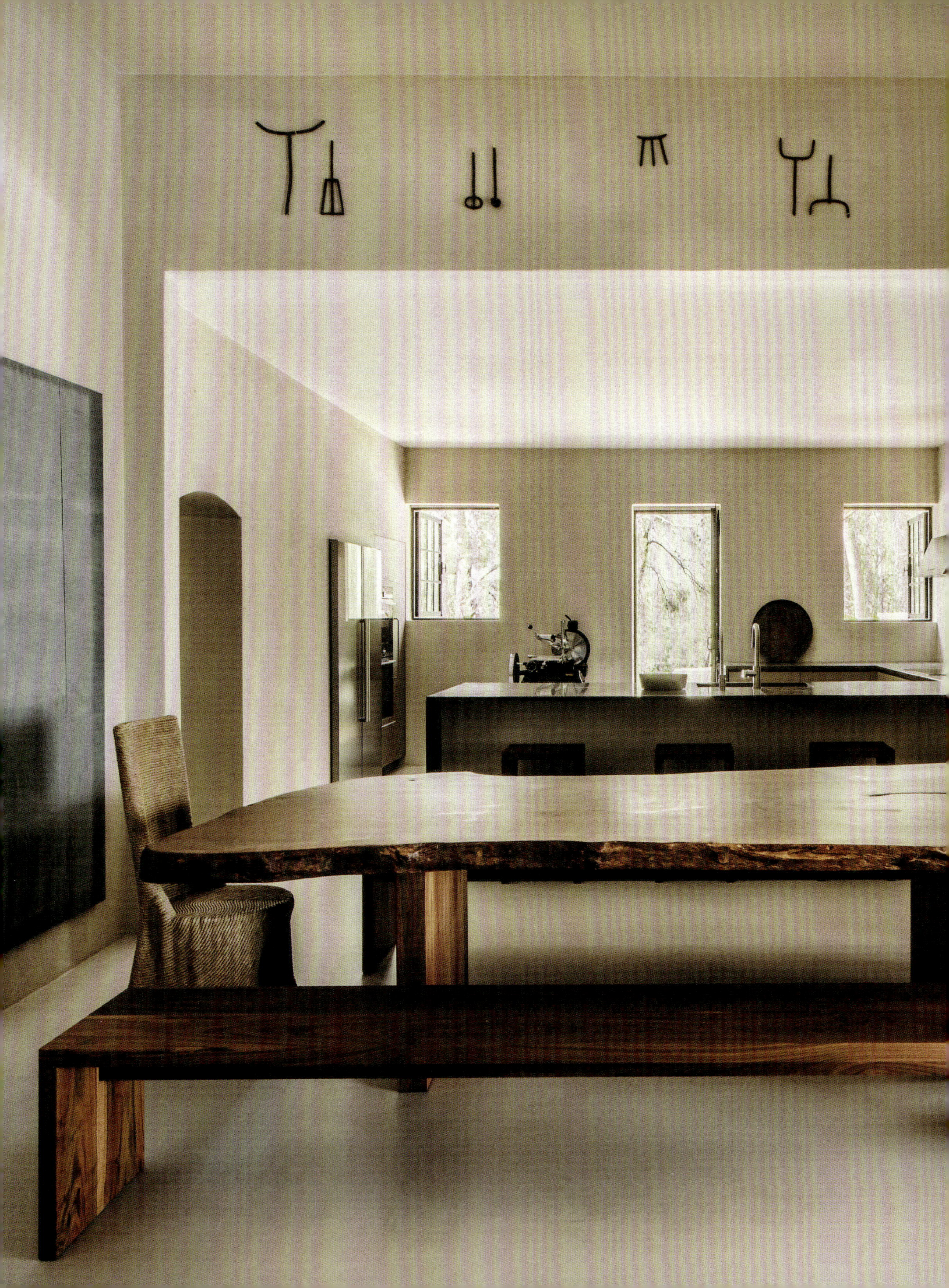

**The form of the house itself and its thick, irregular, lime-plastered walls are incredibly voluptuous, matching perfectly with the sculptural sense the interior designer was aiming for.**

'Sculpture plays a key role in my creative process in general,' Bowden says, 'and approaching this project in a sculptural sense was crucial. The form of the house itself and its thick, irregular, lime-plastered walls are incredibly voluptuous, so I wanted to find counterpoints to balance that. I used pieces like the Natalie Rich-Fernández wall sculptures, or Alexis Gautier embroideries for that rough texture that contrasts with the smooth plaster.'

The entire house is filled with truly unique pieces of furniture and artworks. 'I love the main space and it would be very hard to choose one favourite piece, as I really like everything we chose,' says Bowden. The dining table is truly special; it's three metres long and carved from a single piece of walnut. You can really see the beauty of the grain, and it is bordered with a raw edge that seems to flow like a river into the indigo artwork by Sergej Jensen and a unique moulded chair, draped in hemp rope by Christian Astuguevieille. And I can't not mention the Joe Colombo "Elda" chair. I came across it whilst buying rugs in Morocco, and although in theory its industrial style didn't suit the project, it had been there so many years that the dark brown leather had aged in such a way that the patina gave it a unique character and an appearance very much in keeping with the tone of the project. And so it made the grade!' It's all in the details.

← The dining table is three metres long and carved from a single piece of walnut. Its raw edge that seems to flow like a river into the indigo artwork by Sergej Jensen and a unique hemp rope moulded chair by Christian Astuguevieille

SOBER

The brief was to create a bohemian Ibizan holiday home — serene, unpretentious simplicity with luxurious comfort, a romantic, magical touch, with a great deal of warmth.

A vintage Joe Colombo 'Elda' chair in the living room ←

Serene, unpretentious simplicity with luxurious comfort and a touch of romance and magic ↓

SOBER

→ The house is designed for entertaining, but all of the bedrooms are found at the end of corridors and passages, offering a cosy haven away from the party

SOBER

← The interventions were fairly radical, but the studio used natural materials that soften the sharp edges and sit comfortably within a rather traditional framework

↑
All the materials were chosen specifically for their character and the way they help to enhance what was already there, reflecting their surroundings. Plaster and wood take centre stage, together with the concrete floor

SOBER

← To escape the heat and party atmosphere outside, intimate spaces like the bathrooms are softened with dark tones and dim lighting, creating an ambience of calm and shade

SOBER

# A NEW TAKE ON MINIMALIST

Can a house be both pared-back and at the same time reflect a warm, slightly rustic bohemian style? It can indeed, as this beautiful villa renovated by Hollie Bowden proves so well. A true homage to the maxim 'less is more' with a dash of boho chic.

It's not easy to retain the essence of a house when practically all of the original elements that once defined it are taken away. But London-based interior designer Hollie Bowden has the magic touch, especially when it comes to the typical Ibizan fincas that she knows so well, because she clearly adores the island. So what you see in this villa is another of those little miracles that preserves the best features of the property without sacrificing a renovation that is comprehensive, warm, comfortable and, above all, elegant.

The project was commissioned by a private client with a large family who wanted a place to relax and entertain over the summer. 'The family live between London and Ibiza, so it was designed as a second residence where they could feel just as at home as they did in London,' Bowden explains. 'To create this atmosphere, I made lots of inviting guest rooms and a real bohemian ambience, with multiple textures and layers.' The estate covers 40,000 square metres including buildings and land, is located in the town of Sant Carles, and set within wonderful, sprawling tropical gardens. Its layout includes eight bedrooms, each with a private bathroom, and a sauna, gym, games room and cinema, as well as a large open-plan living room.

The angular architecture and hotchpotch layout provided unique opportunities when developing the design scheme, which meant that the bones of the house have remained intact, although everything else has disappeared. 'We needed to create a house with a broken floor plan, opening up the dining room space so it connected seamlessly with the outside,' explains the designer. 'There is an open flow through the property, as well as cosy and intimate corners to chill out. I wanted to create a relaxed, lived-in, bohemian atmosphere. Everything was painted white, and the stucco walls helped to bring out the depth of the wooden beams.

'To emphasise the contrast in materials of the walls and beams, we stained the latter dark. In general, the project presents organic, natural and earthy materials. I kept the environment quite austere and minimal in terms of furniture and decorative pieces. We respected the

*The angular architecture and hotchpotch layout provided unique opportunities when developing the design scheme, and the corridors and walls are punctuated with handcrafted pieces that emphasise the project's traditional character*

> 'We needed to create a house with a broken floor plan, opening up the dining room space so it connected seamlessly with the outside.'

→→ The aim was to create a house with a broken floor plan, opening up the dining room space so that it connected seamlessly with the outside. The house features a great deal of wood, reworked metal and terracotta

→ The project showcases organic, natural, earthy materials, and the environment was kept quite austere and minimal in terms of furniture and decorative pieces. The basic design was respected, and the ceiling stayed, but everything else changed

basic design and kept the ceiling, but everything else changed. Now, the limestone tiles add a new texture to the scheme and give it even more diversity. If I'm asked how I would describe the style of the house, I would say it has a serene, eclectic and very well-travelled atmosphere. I wanted it to embody the spirit of the people who would be spending time here, strolling barefoot through the gardens. It is deliciously earthy, relaxed and completely unique. I travelled all over Europe in search of one-off vintage pieces and antiques to give the spaces a real authenticity. The house feels full of life but serene at the same time.'

As with all her work, Bowden has used a great deal of wood, reworked metal and terracotta, all of which have aged beautifully, developing wonderful patina. And, of course, she has collaborated with local artisans, something that characterises her projects. 'The curtains are made of raw hemp and linens from the island, and for the hardware we commissioned curtain poles from a local blacksmith.' Added to this incredible world inside is the outside, a lush tropical environment that the designer tried to bring into the house: 'I kept the window treatments minimal to accentuate the gardens and allow the greenery to enter the space, following the earthy palette, and in harmony with the surroundings.'

↑
To create a relaxed, lived-in, bohemian feel, everything was painted white, while the stucco walls helped to bring out the depth of the wooden beams, as here in the bedroom

SOBER

← In some spaces, like the bathroom, the beams were stained dark to contrast with the white walls and grey limestone flooring

253

# CREDITS

### OUT OF THE BLUE
PP. 10—19
**Interior design** Oscar Lucien Ono
@oscarlucien.ono
Maison Numéro 20
maisonnumero20.fr
@maisonnumero20
**Photography by** Francis Amiand
francisamiand.com
@francisamiand

### STARTING FROM SCRATCH
PP. 6, 8 & 20—33
**Architect** Bruno Erpicum
**Interior design and decoration**
Ali Pittam, Can Can Design
@cancandesign_
and Roberta Jurado, Box3 Interiores
@box3ibiza
**Stylist** Amaya de Toledo
**Photography by** Manolo Yllera
www.manoloyllera.com
@manoloyllera

### ADAPT AND THRIVE
PP. 34—47
**Architect and Interior design**
Romano Arquitectos
www.romano.archi
@romanoarquitectos
**Stylist** Amaya de Toledo
**Photography by** Manolo Yllera
www.manoloyllera.com
@manoloyllera

### COOL, CALM AND COLLECTED
PP. 48—55
**Architect & Interior design**
TG-Studio - Thomas Griem
www.tg-studio.co.uk
@tgstudioltd
**Photography by** Philip Vile
philipvile.com
@philipvile

### A PLACE OF ONE'S OWN
PP. 56 & 58—71
**Owner** Francesca Munizaga
@thefarmibiza
@thefarmersclubibiza
PP. 64, 66, 67, 70
**Photography by** Maria Primo
©MARIA PRIMO STUDIO
mariaprimo.com
@mariaprimo
PP. 58, 60, 62, 65, 68, 69, 71
**Photography by** Daniel Balda
danielbalda.com

### A CAREFULLY CRAFTED CASA
PP. 72—81
**Interior design** Alfons & Damian Studio
www.alfonsdamian.com
@alfonsdamian_interiorismo
**Photography by** Eugeni Pons
www.eugenipons.com
@eugenipons

### BETWEEN TWO SEAS
PP. 82—91
**Interior design** Ksar Living
by Alberto Cortes
ksarliving.com
@ksarliving
Yvonne Sophie Hulst
Es Vedrà Bay Villas
esvedrabayvillas.com
**Photography by** Conrad White

### HOME AT LAST
PP. 92 & 94—105
**Owner & Interior design** Sarah Crook
@sarahjcrook
**Photography by** Montse Garriga
montsegarriga.com
@capdemar

### A SENSE OF CRAFT
PP. 106—117
**Owner** Victoria Allan
@victorialallan
**Photography by** Ariadna Puigdomenech
www.ariadnapuigdomenech.com
@aripuigdomenech

### THE GREAT OUTDOORS
PP. 118—129
**Owner** Deborah Brett
www.dbceramic.co.uk
@deborahbrett
@dbceramic
**Photography by** Ana Lui
analuiphotography.com
@analuiphotography

### THE ESSENCE OF IBIZA STYLE
PP. 130—139
**Interior design** Bloom Studio
www.thisisbloomstudio.com
@bloomstudioibiza
**Photography by** Sofia Gomez
sofiagomezfonzo.com
@sofiagomezfonzo

### OLD MEETS NEW
PP. 140–145
**Interior design** Bloom Studio
www.thisisbloomstudio.com
@bloomstudioibiza
**Photography by** Sofia Gomez
sofiagomezfonzo.com
@sofiagomezfonzo

### FROM MIAMI TO IBIZA
PP. 148–153
**Owner** Caroline Legrand
**Interior design** Caroline Legrand
carolinelegranddesign.com
@carolinelegranddesign
**Photography by** Kate Martin
katemartinphotography.co.uk
@katemartinphoto

### URBAN OASIS
PP. 154–159
**Interior design** Caroline Legrand
carolinelegranddesign.com
@carolinelegranddesign
**Photography by** Kate Martin
katemartinphotography.co.uk
@katemartinphoto

### MOORISH MEETS DISCO
PP. 146 & 160–169
**Owner** Jasmien Hamed & Kourosh Ghadishah
tresnomadmaison.com
@stylistjasmine
**Photography by** Rebekka Eliza
www.rebekkaeliza.com
@rebekkaeliza_photographer

### THE WORK OF A LIFETIME
PP. 172–183
**Owner** Luis Galliussi
luisgalliussi.com
@can.kaki
@luisgalliussi
**Photography by** Ricardo Labougle
www.ricardolabougle.com
@ricardolabougle

### SEVENTIES CHIC
PP. 170 & 184–193
**Architect** Rolf BlaKStad
@blakstadibiza
**Photography by** Montse Garriga
montsegarriga.com
@capdemar

### THE BEAT GOES ON
PP. 194–203
**Owner** Laura Martínez and Diego Calvo
@itslauraboyd
@diegocalvoibiza
**Photography by** Xabi Goitisolo
xabigoitisolo.eu
@xabigoitisolo

### A SLICE OF BRAZILIAN MID-CENTURY STYLE
PP. 204–213
**Architect & designer** Natalia Miyar
nataliamiyar.com
**Photography by** Ana Lui
analuiphotography.com
@analuiphotography

### BLENDING INTO THE LANDSCAPE
PP. 214 & 216–229
**Architect & Interior design** Framework Studio
www.framework.eu
@frmwrkstudio
**Photography by** Thomas de Bruyne
@cafeine

### LOOKING BACK, LOOKING EAST
PP. 230–235
**Interior design** El Contempo
elcontempo.com
@elcontempo
**Photography by** Ariadna Puigdomenech
www.ariadnapuigdomenech.com
@aripuigdomenech

### EARTHY DELIGHTS
PP. 236–245
**Design Studio** Hollie Bowden
holliebowden.com
@holliebowden
**Photography by** Genevieve Lutkin
www.genevievelutkin.com
@genevievelutkin

### A NEW TAKE ON MINIMALIST
PP. 246–253
**Design Studio** Hollie Bowden
holliebowden.com
@holliebowden
**Photography by** Genevieve Lutkin
www.genevievelutkin.com
@genevievelutkin

**Concept & Design:** Carolina Amell
**Texts:** Gala Mora
**Translation:** Faye Williams
**Editing:** Léa Teuscher

**Cover photo** by Francis Amiand
**Back cover photos** by Francis Amiand (left), Thomas de Bruyne (top), Montse Garriga (bottom middle) and Manolo Yllera (bottom right)

Sign up for our newsletter with news about new and forthcoming publications on art, interior design, food & travel, photography and fashion as well as exclusive offers and events. If you have any questions or comments about the material in this book, please do not hesitate to contact our editorial team: art@lannoo.com

©Lannoo Publishers, Belgium, 2023
D/2023/45/243 – NUR450/454
ISBN 978 94 014 8936 2
www.lannoo.com

All rights reserved. No part of this publication may be reproduced or transmitted in any form or by any means, electronic or mechanical, including photography, recording or any other information storage and retrieval system, without prior permission in writing from the publisher.

Every effort has been made to trace copyright holders. If, however, you feel that you have inadvertently been overlooked, please contact the publishers.